Every thoughtful Christian ought to read this classic exposition of evangelical essentials. Though written more than forty years ago, its central message stands and is needed today more than ever. John Stott expounds persuasively, generously, lucidly, and with penetrating insight, what it means to be faithful to Jesus Christ. This is a brilliant book.
Christopher Ash, Director of Cornhill Training Course

I vividly recall reading this book in its earliest version forty years ago, and it contained the stand-out set of arguments that persuaded me to commit my life to Christ later that year. Thank you, John, for all that has meant to me since.
Dr Andrew Fergusson, author and former Head of Communications, Christian Medical Fellowship

This is, I believe, not only one of John Stott's finest books, but one of the most important to be written in recent decades. In a world which increasingly rejects the concept of truth, and a church often marked by doctrinal indifference, its appeal to submit to Christ's teaching concerning core convictions and his example in arguing for them is urgently needed.
Vaughan Roberts, Rector of St Ebbes, Oxford, and Director of the Proclamation Trust

This is vintage Stott – clear, biblical, passionate, thoughtful and Christ-centred. A magisterial defence of biblical historic evangelical Christianity. By brilliant analysis of the debates of Jesus with the Pharisees and Sadducees of his day, he highlights modern versions of the same distortions. Profound, lucid and compelling, this book is as relevant to current debates as when it was first published.
John Wyatt, Emeritus Professor of Neonatal Paediatrics at University College London

'But I Say to You . . .'
Christ the controversialist

INTER-VARSITY PRESS
36 Causton Street, London SW1P 4ST, England
Email: ivp@ivpbooks.com
Website: www.ivpbooks.com

First published as Christ the Controversialist *1970*
Published in this format 2013
This edition 2021

British Library Cataloguing-in-Publication Data
A catalogue record for this book is available from the British Library.

ISBN: 978–1–78974–286–2

Set in Adobe Garamond 11.5/15pt
Typeset in Great Britain by CRB Associates, Potterhanworth, Lincolnshire
Printed in Great Britain by Ashford Colour Press Ltd, Gosport, Hampshire

Produced on paper from sustainable forests.

Inter-Varsity Press publishes Christian books that are true to the Bible and that communicate the gospel, develop discipleship and strengthen the church for its mission in the world.

IVP originated within the Inter-Varsity Fellowship, now the Universities and Colleges Christian Fellowship, a student movement connecting Christian Unions in universities and colleges throughout Great Britain, and a member movement of the International Fellowship of Evangelical Students. Website: www.uccf.org.uk. That historic association is maintained, and all senior IVP staff and committee members subscribe to the UCCF Basis of Faith.

All the royalties from this book have been irrevocably assigned to Langham Literature. Langham Literature is a ministry of Langham Partnership, founded by John Stott. Chris Wright is the International Ministries Director.

Langham Literature provides Majority World preachers, scholars and seminary libraries with evangelical books and electronic resources through publishing and distribution, grants and discounts. They also foster the creation of indigenous evangelical books in many languages through writers' grants, strengthening local evangelical publishing houses and investment in major regional literature projects.

For further information on Langham Literature, and the rest of Langham Partnership, visit the website at <www.langham.org>.

JOHN STOTT
1 O O

2021 is the centenary of John Stott's birth. IVP is delighted to celebrate the timeless wisdom and continuing relevance of Stott's teaching. We are pleased to mark the Stott 100 celebrations alongside the organizations he founded, his other publishers and his literary executors.

To find out more about Stott's life, teaching and continuing impact, please visit <johnstott100.org>, or find out more at <ivpbooks.com/Stott100>.

CONTENTS

Foreword 8

Preface 10

FOUNDATIONS

A. A call for clarity 15

B. Why 'evangelical'? 26

CHAPTERS

1. Religion: Natural or supernatural? 43

2. Authority: Tradition or Scripture? 61

3. The Bible: End or means? 80

4. Salvation: Merit or mercy? 97

5. Morality: Outward or inward? 122

6. Worship: Lips or heart? 153

7. Responsibility: Withdrawal or involvement? 167

8. Ambition: Our glory or God's? 185

   Postscript: Jesus, our Teacher and Lord 202

   Notes 209

FOREWORD

It was as a first-year student in 1970 that I first read this penetrating book. I entered a world that was entirely new to me, confronted by a university chaplain who had a very different view of the Bible, by religious groups that were hostile to the claim of the uniqueness of Christ, and by fellow evangelicals who struggled to work together because of controversies over secondary issues. Stott's writing was a shaft of light for a rather confused fresher.

Stott described the spirit of the age, but it is striking that, rereading the book over forty years later, it is even more relevant today. His remarkable foresight has been seen in many of the initiatives he launched, now bearing fruit around the world. But it is also evident in this book, including his anticipation of the intolerance of tolerance, the march of secularization, the engagement of a more confident Islam, the challenges to biblical fidelity in the church, the loss of the centrality of the cross of Christ, and the need for evangelicals to live the truth as well as to believe it.

So for a new day, there is still *an urgent need to confront*. Evangelicals now live in an atmosphere of philosophical pluralism, where sustaining our convictions regarding evangelical truth is more and more demanding. In most corners of the world, now including the West, there is overtly anti-Christian propaganda across the media. Within the Christian community, the loss of Christo-centricity and biblical literacy is typical of the big challenges confronting the health and growth of the church.

Not only so, there is *a need to confront wisely*. Stott's writing helps us to identify more precisely which battles must be fought and which issues need to be clarified. He deftly indicates which issues are primary, and which can be laid aside. And in case we should imagine we will always find ourselves on the right side of the controversy, we might find Stott's perceptive biblical insights and application will also serve as a critique of some aspects of contemporary evangelicalism too.

And further, there is *a need to confront graciously*. Stott became known worldwide not only as a remarkably courageous and articulate defender of evangelical truth, but also as a man of great humility and grace. One of the special values of this title is that it models the way in which Christians should engage with controversy, and this is surely needed at a time when evangelical voices are often too shrill and strident, when the manner of our defence of the truth sometimes gives the lie to our commitment to that truth. I have often been struck by the way Stott exemplified the great leadership quality of being a man with a tough mind and a tender heart.

As in the first edition, this book carries a typically self-effacing prayer in its Preface: 'that God will forgive its imperfections, overruling what it contains of error that it may bring harm to no-one and owning what it contains of truth that it may bring blessing to some'. Since Stott penned those words, hundreds of thousands of believers have benefitted enormously from his writing and his personal example, and so we pray that its re-release will bring blessing to a new generation of readers around the world.

Jonathan Lamb
Director, Langham Preaching
Oxford, UK
May 2013

PREFACE

The title for the original edition of this book was 'Christ the Controversialist'. John Stott's intention was to indicate not that Jesus Christ was a controversial figure, but that he engaged in controversy. Much of Christ's public speaking took the form of debates with the contemporary Palestinian leaders of religion. They did not agree with him, and he did not agree with them.

John Stott's aim in studying these controversies of Christ was to clarify the issues being debated, to demonstrate that they were the live issues in 1970 that they continue to be today, and to argue that the position which Christ adopted in each debate is the very position which 'evangelical' Christians have always sought to maintain. He explained why he believed this exercise to be necessary in two introductory chapters, which we have called Foundations.

In the first he sought to defend the task of theological definition. It was an unpopular task when he first wrote about it and remains so today. The non-Christian world is saturated with the spirit of pragmatism and owns up to being sick of the church's unpractical theologizing. And in some parts of today's church the same spirit prevails. Many have given up any hope of doctrinal certainty, let alone of doctrinal agreement. John Stott tried therefore to unearth the roots of this hostility to theological definition, and to argue that we must still pursue and not abandon the task.

In the second Foundation chapter he made a plea for 'evangelical' Christianity. That is, having underlined the need for theological definition, he went on to urge that we must define

Christianity 'evangelically'. His concern was with truth, and in particular with the doctrinal position held by so-called 'evangelical' Christians. What name we take or others give us is a trivial question in comparison with the great doctrines by which we seek to live, and whether or not they are true. The doctrines we hold are commonly known as 'the evangelical faith'. Whether it is correct to use this phrase isn't really the issue. What matters is the substance, not the style. And the substance, John Stott claimed, is biblical, original, fundamental Christianity. He believed (with conviction and, he hoped, with humility) that this faith is the true faith of Christ, as he taught it to his apostles and especially as he defended it against its opponents and detractors.

The chapters which follow the Foundations are devoted to a consideration of Christ's controversies. John Stott did not attempt an exhaustive treatment of them, but concentrated on the major topics of debate which (it seemed to him) were dominant in Christ's day and still are now. He chose to consider, therefore, such basic questions as the character of the Christian's God and of the Christian religion, the authority and purpose of Scripture, the way of salvation, the kind of morality and worship which are acceptable to God, the nature of Christian responsibility and of Christian ambition. On each of these matters Jesus Christ disagreed with the teaching of either the Pharisees or the Sadducees, and on each matter 'evangelical' Christians are in disagreement with others in today's church. Indeed, so John Stott's argument runs, when we put together the truths on which Christ insisted in these controversies, the result is a fairly comprehensive exposition of what is meant by 'evangelical religion'.

The theme of this book lingered and matured in John Stott's mind over a number of years. He took it for a series of sermons in All Souls Church in 1962 and again, further developed, in 1968/9. He also gave a series of popular lectures under the title 'Christ the Controversialist' both in Edinburgh in November 1968 (for the Edinburgh Evangelical Council) and in Auckland in May 1969 (for the New Zealand Evangelical Alliance).

Convinced of the book's enduring relevance, John Stott's Literary Executors are glad to reissue it in this new edition. We are grateful to Canon David Stone for his skilful work in editing the text for the twenty-first century. In doing this, some applications that would now be of only historical interest have been omitted. We have been careful, however, not to omit or dilute any of the author's challenges to Christian thought or practice. Nor have we introduced new material, which would have involved guessing how he might interact with issues or writers today.

We echo what John Stott wrote in the original preface: 'I now send the book on its way with the earnest prayer that God will forgive its imperfections, overruling what it contains of error that it may bring harm to no-one and owning what it contains of truth that it may bring blessing to some.'

FOUNDATIONS

A

A call for clarity

The aim of this book is simple. It is to argue that 'evangelical' Christianity is real Christianity – authentic, true, original and pure – and to show this from the teaching of Jesus Christ himself.

Such an attempt to explain and to establish a particular brand of Christianity will not be welcomed by everyone – far from it! So let me therefore try at once to anticipate some possible criticisms.

1. Dislike of dogmatism

The first objection to the theme of this book will stem from a dislike of dogmatism. The spirit of our age is hostile towards people who state their opinions clearly and hold them strongly. Someone of conviction, however intelligent, sincere and humble they may be, is likely to labelled a bigot. Nowadays the really great mind is thought to be both broad and open – broad enough to absorb every fresh idea which is presented to it, and open enough to go on doing so for ever.

In reply to this, we need to say that the Christian Faith is essentially dogmatic, because it claims to be a *revealed* Faith. If Christianity were just a collection of human ideas, then dogmatic certainty would be entirely out of place. But if (as Christians claim) God has spoken – both long ago through the prophets and in these last days through his Son[1] – what is wrong with believing what he has said and urging other people to believe it too? If there is a Word from God which may be read and received today, it would surely be both foolish and wrong to ignore it.

Of course the fact that God has spoken, and that what he has said is recorded in a book, does not mean that Christians know everything. We may sometimes give the impression that we think we do – in which case we need to be forgiven for our arrogance. As the apostle John makes clear in his first letter, for example, 'what we will be has not yet been made known'.[2] Back in the Old Testament, Moses was someone to whom God revealed himself to an extraordinary degree. Yet he was quite clear that God had only *begun* 'to show to your servant your greatness . . . '[3] Along the same lines the apostle Paul likened our present and partial knowledge to the ignorant chatter of a child.[4] If Moses in the Old Testament, and John and Paul in the New, humbly admit their ignorance of so much truth, who are we to claim that we know it all? We need to hear again the sobering words of Jesus: 'It is not for you to know . . . '[5] He was referring to the times and dates 'which the Father has set by his own authority'. But the same principle applies in other areas of truth. The limits of our knowledge are set, not by what we decide we want to know, but by what God has decided to reveal to us.

Perhaps the most balanced statement of this comes towards the end of the Old Testament book of Deuteronomy: 'The secret things belong to the LORD our God, but the things revealed belong to us and to our children for ever . . . '[6] Here the sum total of truth is divided into two parts, 'the secret things' and 'the things revealed'. We are told that the secret things belong to God. And since they belong to him and he has not decided to pass them on to us, we should not attempt to force them from him but be content to leave them with him. The revealed things, on the other hand, 'belong to us and to our children for ever'. That is, since God has given them to us and they are ours, he means us to possess them ourselves and to hand them on to the next generation. God's purpose, therefore, is for us to enjoy what is ours (because he has revealed it), and not to worry about what is his alone (because he has not revealed it).

We are to be clear about what has been plainly revealed and to admit our ignorance about what has not; and it is this Christian combination of dogmatism and agnosticism which we find so hard to get right. Problems arise when we allow our dogmatism to invade the territory of 'the secret things' or our agnosticism to obscure 'the things that are revealed'. We need to be able to tell the difference between these two areas of truth, the secret and the revealed. It is as much a sign of maturity to say 'I don't know' about one thing as it is to say 'I know' about another – provided that our admission of ignorance is about something kept secret and our claim to knowledge about something revealed.

So Christian dogmatism is (or should be) limited. It is very far from being a claim to know everything. But when it comes to what is clearly revealed in the Bible, Christians should be neither doubtful nor apologetic. The New Testament reverberates with clear affirmations beginning 'We know', 'We are sure', 'We are confident'. Just have a look at the first Letter of John, in which verbs meaning 'to know' occur about forty times. They strike a note of joyful assurance which is sadly missing from many parts of the church today and which needs to be recaptured. As Professor James Stewart has written, 'It is quite mistaken to suppose that humility excludes conviction. G. K. Chesterton once penned some wise words about what he called "the dislocation of humility" . . . "What we suffer from today is humility in the wrong place."[7]

What he means is that we should admit our limitations when it comes to understanding truth but not doubt the reality of the truth itself. The problem is that this has been exactly reversed. As Chesterton says, 'We are on the road to producing a race of people too mentally modest to believe in the multiplication table.' 'Humble and self-forgetting we must be always,' Professor Stewart continues, 'but diffident and apologetic about the Gospel never.' The dictionary which defined dogma as an 'arrogant declaration of opinion' got it wrong. Being dogmatic does not necessarily mean being either proud or opinionated.

In other words, a broad and open mind, valued so highly in our day, is not necessarily a good thing. To be sure, we must keep an *open* mind about matters on which the Bible seems to be unclear, and a *receptive* mind so that our understanding of God's revelation can continue to deepen. We must also distinguish between the essence of a doctrine and our imperfect ways of understanding and stating it. But when the teaching of the Bible is plain, then continuing to maintain an open mind is a sign not of maturity, but of immaturity. Those who cannot make up their minds what to believe, who are 'blown here and there by every wind of teaching', are labelled by Paul as 'infants'.[8] And having people who are 'always learning but never able to come to a knowledge of the truth'[9] is a characteristic of the 'terrible times' in which we are living.

2. Hatred of controversy
The second way in which the spirit of the age is hostile towards the theme of this book is the modern hatred of controversy.

That is to say, it is bad enough to be dogmatic, we are told. But 'if you must be dogmatic', our critics continue, 'do at least keep your dogmatism to yourself. Hold your own definite convictions (if you must), but leave other people alone in theirs. Be tolerant. Mind your own business, and let the rest of the world mind theirs.'

Another way in which this point of view is expressed is to urge us always to be positive, if necessary dogmatically positive, but never to be negative. 'Speak up for what you believe,' we are told, 'but don't speak against what other people believe.' The Bible's problem with this approach is that the Christian leader is not only to 'encourage by sound doctrine' but also to 'refute those who oppose it'.[10]

Opposition to intolerance arises naturally from a dislike of dogmatism. Indeed, the two usually go together. It is very easy to tolerate the opinions of others if we have no strong opinions of our own. But this is not something we should go along with. We need to make a distinction between the tolerant mind and the tolerant spirit. A Christian should always be tolerant in *spirit* – loving, understanding, forgiving and being patient with others, making allowances for them, and giving them the benefit of the doubt, for true love 'always protects, always trusts, always hopes, always perseveres'.[11] But how can we be tolerant in *mind* of what God has clearly revealed to be wrong?

Certainly every right-thinking person will avoid unnecessary controversy, and we should steer clear of argument for argument's sake. 'Don't have anything to do with foolish and stupid arguments,' wrote the apostle Paul, 'because you know they produce quarrels.'[12] There's something wrong with us if we relish controversy. We should hesitate before getting involved in an argument. We must also be careful to avoid any trace of bitterness. Controversy conducted in a hostile way, which descends to personal insult and abuse, stains all too many of the pages of church history. But we cannot avoid controversy itself. 'Defending and confirming the gospel'[13] is part of what God calls us to do.

Perhaps the best way to back up the claim that controversy is sometimes a painful necessity is to remember that our Lord Jesus Christ himself was a controversialist. He was not 'broad-minded' in the sense that he was prepared to go along with any views on any subject. On the contrary, as we will see in the later chapters of this book, he frequently engaged in debate with the religious leaders of his day, the teachers of the law and Pharisees, the Herodians and Sadducees. He claimed that he himself was the truth, that he had come to testify to the truth, and that the truth would set his followers free.[14] His loyalty to the truth meant that he was not afraid to disagree publicly with official pronouncements (if he knew them to be wrong), to expose error, and to warn his disciples about false teachers.[15] He was also extremely outspoken in his language, calling them 'blind guides', 'wolves in sheep's clothing', 'whitewashed tombs' and even a 'brood of vipers'.[16]

It wasn't only Jesus himself. The New Testament Letters make it clear that the apostles were controversialists too. Jude, for example, appealed to his readers 'to contend for the faith that was once for all entrusted to God's holy people'.[17] Like their Lord and Master, they needed to warn the churches of false teachers and to urge them to stand firm in the truth.

It's sometimes suggested that this is incompatible with love. But take John, for example, well-known as the apostle of love. We have from him the sublime declaration that God is love, and his letters overflow with appeals for Christians to love one another. Yet he roundly declares that whoever denies that Jesus is the Christ is a liar, a deceiver and antichrist.[18] Similarly

Paul, who in 1 Corinthians 13 gives us the great hymn to love, and declares that love is the supreme hallmark of the Spirit, nonetheless pronounces a solemn curse upon anyone who distorts the gospel of the grace of God.[19]

In our generation we seem to have moved a long way from this vigorous passion for the truth displayed by Christ and his apostles. But if we loved the glory of God more, and if we cared more for the eternal good of other people, we would surely be more ready to engage in controversy when the truth of the gospel is at stake. The command is clear. We are to 'maintain the truth in love'[20] – being neither truthless in our love, nor loveless in our truth, but holding the two in balance.

3. The call to close our ranks

A third argument against the attempt to define the Christian Faith too clearly or too narrowly is based on the situation in our world today. We are reminded that the church in the West is steadily losing ground in many places. Not only is the population explosion outstripping the conversion rate, but forces opposed to Christianity are growing stronger. In some areas Islam claims to be winning more converts than Christianity. The ancient religions of the East are experiencing a revival in a number of countries where, together with a passionate commitment to nationalism, Christianity is dismissed as the religion of unwanted foreigners. Then there is the strong current of secularism in the modern world, sucking individuals and societies into its powerful vortex. Surely, it is said, in face of this menace to the Christian religion, we must close ranks. We can no longer afford the luxury of division. We are fighting for our very survival.

This appeal for unity is a moving one, and we should not ignore it. It contains much with which we entirely agree. Some of our divisions are not only unnecessary, but an offence to God and a hindrance to the spread of the gospel. I believe that the visible unity of the church is both biblically right and practically desirable, and that we should be actively seeking it. At the same time, we need to ask ourselves a simple but searching question. If we are to meet those who oppose Christ with a united Christian front, what kind of Christianity are we going to promote? The only weapon with which the opponents of the gospel can be overcome is the gospel itself. It would be a tragedy if we were to abandon the only effective weapon in our armoury. United Christianity which is not true Christianity will not gain the victory over non-Christian forces, but will be defeated by them.

4. The spirit of ecumenism

The fourth contemporary influence which is unfriendly towards the theme of this book is the spirit of ecumenism. In saying this, I have no intention of condemning the efforts of those in the ecumenical movement to draw Christians closer to one another. On the contrary, much that has been achieved in mutual understanding and in projects such as Christian Aid is right and good. I am trying rather to describe what may perhaps be called 'the ecumenical outlook'. According to this point of view, no individual or church has a monopoly of the truth. Instead, all Christians, whatever their opinions, have their own 'insights' into the truth and therefore their own 'contribution' to make to the common life of the church. Those who take this view look forward to the day when all Christians and churches will come together and pool what they have to offer. Many see the resulting mix, hard as it is to imagine, as the ultimate goal. With an outlook like this, the evangelical desire to define some truths in such a way as to exclude others can only be seen as misguided and damaging.

The right approach of Christians who disagree with one another is neither to ignore, nor to conceal, nor even to minimize their differences, but to debate them. Take the Roman Catholic Church as an example. I find it distressing to see Protestants and Roman Catholics united in a common act of worship or witness. Why? Because it gives the onlooker the impression that their disagreements are now virtually over. 'See,' the ordinary person on the street might say, 'they can now take part in prayer and proclamation together; why are they still divided?'

But such a public display of unity is a game of let's pretend; it is not living in the real world. Certainly we can be very thankful for the signs of a loosening rigidity and of a greater biblical awareness in the Roman Catholic Church. In consequence, many individual Roman Catholics have come to embrace more biblical truth than they had previously grasped, and some have felt it right to leave their church. The reforms of recent years have so let the Bible loose in the church that no-one can guess what the final result may be. We pray that under God it will prove to be a thoroughgoing biblical reformation. In some places, however, an alarming opposite tendency is appearing, a theological liberalism as radical as anything to be found in Protestant Christendom. The third possibility is that victory will go to those who oppose the reforms.

We have to recognize that, in keeping with Rome's claim that she is *semper eadem* (always the same), none of her defined dogmas has yet been officially redefined. This follows logically from her claim to infallibility. After all, if an utterance is infallible, it cannot be reformed. At the very least we must say that what restatement or redefinition there has been contains no explicit rejection of any statement or definition of the past. There has been no public acknowledgment of past sins and errors, even though this, for a church as for an individual, is an

essential condition of reconciliation. Instead, contemporary
Roman pronouncements swing between the progressive and the
conservative, expressing the painful inner tensions of the church.
Occasionally a word of encouragement is spoken which raises
one's hopes that Rome is going to allow the Bible to judge and
reform it. And then this flickering hope is snuffed out by a
statement which seems to go back to where we began.

What is needed between Protestants and Roman Catholics
is not a premature outward show of unity, but a candid and
serious 'dialogue'. Some Protestants regard such conversation
with Roman Catholics as going too far, but it need not be
so. The Greek verb from which dialogue comes is used in the
Acts for reasoning with people by using the Scriptures. Its
purpose for the Protestants is twofold: first, that by careful
listening they may understand what Roman Catholics are
saying, and thereby avoid mere shadow-boxing, and secondly,
that they may witness plainly and firmly to biblical truth as they
have been given to see it.

The essential thing in such dialogue is that we know exactly
what we are talking about. Two people cannot understand each
other's convictions if they have not first taken time and trouble
to express clearly what they themselves believe. Much discussion
is doomed to failure from the start because of this very lack of
understanding. There are many who prefer to fight their intellectual battles in what Dr Francis L. Patton has aptly called a
'condition of low visibility': What is needed is more defining of
terms, not less. This is the only way to clear the fog.

Dislike of dogmatism, hatred of controversy, love of tolerance,
the call to close our ranks, and the spirit of ecumenism – these
are some of the modern tendencies which are unfriendly to the
purpose of this book. But the Christian church, both universal
and local, is intended by God to be a confessional church. The

church is 'the pillar and foundation of the truth'.[21] Paul pictures revealed truth as a building, and the church's calling is to be its 'foundation' (holding it firm so that it is not moved) and its 'pillar' (holding it high so that all may see it). However hostile the spirit of the age may be to an outspoken statement of the truth, the church has no freedom to reject its God-given task.

B

Why 'evangelical'?

I have argued above that we must define clearly what we mean by 'Christianity'.

Supposing this were to be agreed, how can we justify defining it in 'evangelical' terms? This is the second initial question which we must consider. In reply to it, I will make (and attempt to defend) four assertions about the word 'evangelical'.

1. Evangelical means theological

People often use the term 'evangelical' as if it were the same as 'evangelistic'. One of my colleagues once received a letter of instructions about a speaking invitation. He was told that, because the members of the group were all Christians, they didn't 'want anything evangelical'! What was meant, of course, was that they were not asking for an *evangelistic* address. But the words 'evangelical' and 'evangelistic' should not be confused. The adjective 'evangelistic' describes an *activity*, that of spreading the gospel. 'Evangelical', on the other hand, describes a *theology*, what the apostle Paul called 'the truth of the gospel'. Ideally, of course, the two words belong together, because they both contain the 'evangel', from the Greek word for gospel. Since, strictly speaking, an 'evangelical' is a person who believes the doctrines of the gospel, and an 'evangelist' is a person who proclaims them, it is hard to see how anybody could be one without the other.

Yet the truth is that 'evangelism' and 'evangelicalism' have often been separated. Some claim to be keen on 'evangelism' while not agreeing with the distinctive ideas associated with 'evangelical' people, while not all 'evangelicals' have been all that obviously keen on 'evangelistic' activity. Be that as it may, this book is concerned not with the practice of 'evangelism' (except briefly in chapter 7) but with 'evangelicalism', the theological convictions of 'evangelical' Christians.

Evangelical doctrine and those who hold it are found in nearly all the Protestant churches. Indeed, evangelical believers often experience deeper fellowship with one another across denominational frontiers, than with non-evangelicals in their own churches. For true fellowship is the fellowship of the gospel, a partnership in believing its truth, enjoying its benefits and making it known to others. It has resulted in the formation of such interdenominational bodies as the Evangelical Alliance in Britain (affiliated to the World Evangelical Fellowship) and the Universities and Colleges Christian Fellowship (affiliated to the International Fellowship of Evangelical Students). It means also that the real difference in Christendom today, at least in Protestant Christendom, is not between Episcopalians and non-Episcopalians (whether Presbyterian or Independent), or between so-called State Churches and Free Churches, but between evangelicals and the rest.

2. Evangelical means biblical

Evangelicals claim to be plain Bible Christians – from which it follows that in order to be a truly biblical Christian it is necessary to be an evangelical Christian. Putting it like this runs the risk of sounding arrogant and exclusive. But our intention is not to be partisan. That is, we do not cling to certain views for the sake of maintaining our identity as a 'party'. On the contrary, evangelicals have always been ready to change, or even abandon, any or all of their cherished beliefs if they can be shown to be unbiblical.

This is why evangelicals regard biblical reformation as the only possible route to the reunion of churches. In their view the only solid hope for churches which desire to unite is a common willingness to sit down together under the authority of God's Word, in order to be judged and reformed by it.

This being so, evangelicals cannot go along with the fashionable ecumenical idea that each church has a fragment of the truth, and that the truth cannot be recovered until all churches add their pieces of truth together. Dr J. I. Packer sums this up with his customary clarity:

> You cannot add to evangelical theology without subtracting from it. By augmenting it, you cannot enrich it; you can only impoverish it. Thus, for example, if you add to it a doctrine of human priestly mediation, you take away the truth of the perfect adequacy of our Lord's priestly mediation. If you add to it a doctrine of human merit, in whatever form, you take away the truth of the perfect adequacy of the merits of Christ . . . The principle applies at point after point. What is more than evangelical is less than evangelical. Evangelical theology, by its very nature, cannot be supplemented; it can only be denied.[1]

This claim that evangelical theology is biblical theology means that it is the theology of the whole Bible. Evangelicals have sometimes been accused of choosing isolated extracts from

Scripture to suit their own convenience. But if and when they
have been guilty of this practice, they have contradicted their
true character and witness. Evangelicals are committed to the
whole of Scripture, as it unfolds what Paul termed 'the whole
will of God'.[2] Indeed, since one important meaning of the
word 'catholic' is 'loyal to the whole truth', I would dare even
to say that, properly understood, the Christian faith, the catholic
faith, the biblical faith and the evangelical faith are one and the
same thing.

3. Evangelical means original

If evangelical theology is biblical theology, it follows that it is
not a new-fangled 'ism', a modern brand of Christianity, but an
ancient form, indeed the original one. It is New Testament
Christianity. More than that, the distinctive doctrines on which
evangelical believers insist are all to be found in the actual
teaching of Jesus himself. This is what I propose to concentrate
on in the later chapters of this book. I hope to show that the
points at issue in Christ's controversies with his contemporaries, notably with the Pharisees and the Sadducees, are still
burning issues today, and that evangelicals are simply trying to
be faithful to the principles which he set out.

The same is true of the apostles. It is our claim that the evangelical faith is the apostolic faith. We accept the unique authority
of the apostles of Jesus Christ and want to submit to their
teaching. We observe that they made their own instruction the
rule by which people's opinions were to be tested. Paul expected
obedience from his readers. He tells the Thessalonians to note
and to avoid anybody who does not live 'according to the
teaching you received from us'[3] and who 'does not obey our
instruction in this letter'.[4] Similarly, John, writing to those
troubled by false teachers, warned them that 'anyone who runs

ahead and does not continue in the teaching of Christ does not have God; whoever continues in the teaching has both the Father and the Son'.[5] It is likely that the false teachers were Gnostics who claimed for themselves a special, esoteric enlightenment. In their opinion they were the advanced thinkers, the progressives. They were not stick-in-the-muds like the common herd of Christians. But John is not impressed by their pretensions. A Christian's duty, he insists, is not to advance but to 'continue', not to 'run ahead' of the apostolic faith but to remain within it.

This appeal of the New Testament authors to their readers to be loyal to the primitive apostolic teaching is frequent and urgent. So that we can feel its cumulative force, let me set out some of its main examples:

Paul: 'So then, brothers and sisters, stand firm and hold fast to the teachings we passed on to you, whether by word of mouth or by letter.'[6]

'Now, brothers and sisters, I want to remind you of the gospel I preached to you, which you received and on which you have taken your stand. By this gospel you are saved, if you hold firmly to the word I preached to you. Otherwise, you have believed in vain.'[7]

'But even if we or an angel from heaven should preach a gospel other than the one we preached to you, let them be under God's curse! As we have already said, so now I say again: If anybody is preaching to you a gospel other than what you accepted, let them be under God's curse!'[8]

'Timothy, guard what has been entrusted to your care.'[9]

'What you heard from me, keep as the pattern of sound teaching . . . Guard the good deposit that was entrusted to you . . . '[10]

'But as for you, continue in what you have learned and have

become convinced of, because you know those from whom you learned it.'[11]

Peter: 'For you have been born again . . . through the living and enduring word of God. For . . . the word of the Lord endures forever. And this is the word that was preached to you.'[12]

'So I will always remind you of these things, even though you know them and are firmly established in the truth you now have. I think it is right to refresh your memory as long as I live in the tent of this body . . . And I will make every effort to see that after my departure you will always be able to remember these things.'[13]

Hebrews: 'We must pay the most careful attention, therefore, to what we have heard, so that we do not drift away.'[14]

Remember your leaders, who spoke the word of God to you. Consider the outcome of their way of life and imitate their faith . . . Do not be carried away by all kinds of strange teachings . . . '[15]

John: 'Dear friends, I am not writing you a new command but an old one, which you have had since the beginning. This old command is the message you have heard.'[16]

'As for you, see that what you have heard from the beginning remains in you. If it does, you also will remain in the Son and in the Father . . . I am writing these things to you about those who are trying to lead you astray.'[17]

Jude: 'Dear friends . . . I felt compelled to write and urge you to contend for the faith that was once for all entrusted to God's holy people.'[18]

Revelation: 'Now I say to the rest of you in Thyatira, to you who do not hold to her teaching [i.e. of 'that woman Jezebel, who calls herself a prophet . . . '] and have not learned Satan's so-called deep secrets, "I will not impose any other burden on you, except to hold on to what you have until I come."'[19]

These passages are impressively unanimous. The writers refer to a certain body of revealed teaching which is variously described as 'the gospel', 'the faith' or (more fully) 'the faith that was once for all entrusted to God's holy people', 'the truth', 'the sound teaching', 'the pattern of sound teaching', 'which you have had since the beginning' and 'the good deposit'. This was the message which the apostles had 'preached', 'passed on' and 'entrusted' to the church, so that the early Christians could be said to have 'heard', 'received', 'learned' and 'believed' it, to 'know' it and 'have' it, to 'stand' in it, to be 'firmly established' in it and to be in the process of being 'saved' by it. Now the New Testament authors write to the churches to 'remind' them of this original message. They urge them to 'remember' it, not to 'drift away' from it but to 'pay the most close attention' to it, to 'stand firm' in it, to 'follow' it, to 'continue' in it and let it 'abide' in them, to 'hold' it fast, to 'guard' it as a precious treasure and to 'contend' for it earnestly against all false teachers.

This constant referring back to the past fills many of our contemporaries with dismay. It seems to them to condemn the Christian church to stagnation and the Christian faith to sterility. We need to move with the times, they say, to be up-to-date in our views, not stuck in the past. We need to be flexible, not set for ever in the same old mould.

Indeed, there has probably never been a generation more suspicious of the old and more confident in the new than our present generation. Our culture is in revolt against what it has inherited from the past (in many cases understandably and justifiably so). It hates tradition and loves revolution. Anything which smacks of rigid institutionalism, of the status quo or of the establishment is just not tolerated.

Such a wholesale rejection of what is old is, to say the least, extremely naïve – though we need at once to add that the opposite tendency of resistance to all change is equally mistaken! Time does not stand still. History is change. Far from impeding progress, for example in scientific discovery and social justice, Christians should be in the forefront of advance. For the Christian church to be reactionary, clinging to intellectual prejudices which are no longer reasonable, defending its entrenched positions of privilege and condoning the inequalities in society, is a major denial of Christ. For such things we deserve to be criticized and need humbly to repent.

The Christian's welcome of change must be discriminating, however. In particular, it does not include the apostolic doctrine we find in the New Testament. Our responsibility here is not to abandon it but to hold it fast, not to modify it but to maintain it in its purity.

Although the 'oldness' of the Christian faith may a stumbling-block to many, it is a stumbling-block which cannot be removed. Christianity is Christ himself, together with the witness of the prophets and apostles to him. It depends on a historical event (the birth, life, death, resurrection, ascension and Spirit-gift of Jesus) and on historical testimony by eyewitnesses. It's obvious that these can't be changed or superseded. We live in the twenty-first century, but we are tethered to the first. What Jesus Christ said and did was unique and final. So is the teaching of the apostles, his chosen eyewitnesses and ambassadors. In him, the Word made flesh, and in what the apostles say about him, God's self-revelation was brought to its completion. This completed revelation, which God has caused to be preserved for us in the Bible, is to be held firmly by the church in every age. It is in this sense that all Christians are (or should be) 'conservative', because it is their duty to conserve the truth which has been handed down to them from Christ and the apostles. In everything else, however – in social and church structures, in patterns of ministry and worship, in Christian living and missionary outreach, and in much else besides – the Christian is duty-bound to be as radical as Scripture commands and is free to be as radical as the Bible allows.

So Christianity is old, and is getting older every year. Yet it is also new, new every morning. As John put it: 'Dear friends, I am not writing you a new command but an old one, which you have had since the beginning . . . Yet I am writing you a new command; its truth is seen in him and in you, because the darkness is passing and the true light is already shining.'[20] What he wrote about the command is equally applicable to the whole of Christianity. It is both old and new at the same time. We have considered its oldness. In what sense is it also new? John's straightforward answer is that it is new because it is true. For what is true is always new. It has about it a timelessness which keeps it constantly fresh. Again, it is new because it belongs to the new age. The darkness (of the old age), John says, is passing away, and the true light (of the new age) is already shining. So whatever belongs to the old age is old; they will pass away together. But whatever belongs to the new age is new; they will remain together forever. We must look into this 'newness' further.

First, the old needs to be *freshly understood*. The fact that God's revelation reached its climax and completion in Christ and in the apostles' teaching about Christ doesn't mean that we have nothing more to learn. The Holy Spirit has continued and still continues to teach the people of God. But his continuing instruction is best seen in terms of illumination, not revelation. Revelation is the historical unveiling of God in Christ; illumination is the unveiling of our minds to see what God has made known in Christ. God intends no new revelation for the church, but rather a growing and deepening understanding of the old.

Indeed, it is precisely this which he has given down the centuries. Step by step, often through painful conflict and controversy, the Holy Spirit of truth has enabled the church to increase its grasp of the biblical faith and so to clarify its belief and message. The history of the church is a history of debate in which the truths of the Bible have been successively defined so as to exclude the opinions of those who have questioned, obscured or denied them. This does not mean, however, that the church's formulations of doctrine (its creeds and confessions) possess the same unalterable infallibility as the scriptural doctrine itself. The ways in which we set out what we believe must be expressed afresh in each generation.

Secondly, the old needs to be *freshly applied*. Christianity is often dismissed as irrelevant. But the fault doesn't lie with Christianity, whose truths and principles have an eternal validity. The problem is the church and our frequent failure to reapply Christian truth to the modern situation. Those who study the Bible carefully are constantly impressed with its relevance for today, a relevance which it is the job of Christian preachers and teachers to demonstrate. Preaching must include how to put Bible truth into practice as well as explaining what it means. To preach is to build bridges between God's never-changing Word and our ever-changing world. The fact that the oldness of Christianity is a stumbling-block to many brings an increased challenge to the church to indicate its true newness by delivering an ever-fresh message from an ancient book.

Thirdly, the old needs to be *freshly experienced*. The Jesus of history is the Christ of faith, whom we know and love, trust and obey. After every fresh experience of the saving power of Christ the Christian can say that he has 'put a new song in my mouth, a hymn of praise to our God'.[21] The truth is that everything old has to be freshened if it is to remain new. Old silver needs to be polished, old friendships kept in good repair, old memories revived, old resolutions repeated and (in the same way) old truths recovered.

Every Christian knows the tendency to spiritual staleness. Only by a fresh understanding and appreciation of our inheritance in Christ can the old faith be experienced as new by us and be communicated as new to others. As P. T. Forsyth expressed it, the preacher 'must be original in the sense that his truth is his own, but not in the sense that it has been no-one else's. You must distinguish between novelty and freshness. The preacher is not to be original in the sense of being absolutely *new*, but in the sense of being *fresh*, of appropriating for his own personality, or his own age, what is the standing possession of the Church, and its perennial trust from Christ.'[22]

The history of the church has been tarnished by a repeated failure to hold together the oldness and the newness of the Christian Faith. Sometimes it has successfully maintained the old faith, but failed to relate it to the new world. At other times it has been determined to communicate with the new world, but failed in the process to preserve the old faith in its purity. We have thought about how what is old must be freshly grasped and applied; we must now emphasize the need, while striving to speak relevantly to the modern world, to remain loyal to the old, the original, the apostolic faith.

Every true reform movement has involved a return at some point to the pattern set out for us in the New Testament. The most notable example is the sixteenth-century Reformation, which was a radical attempt under God to purge the church of its medieval additions and corruptions. The Reformers understood their task quite clearly. They were neither destroyers of the past nor inventors of the future. Their ambition was to reform the church by shaping it to the requirements of God's Word. As

Bishop Lancelot Andrewes was to say at the beginning of the seventeenth century, 'we are renovators not innovators'.[23]

It is particularly interesting to note that their recovery of original New Testament truth was nevertheless condemned by their opponents as a dangerous innovation. This was a charge which they vigorously denied, asserting that it was their challengers who were the innovators. Thus, Martin Luther could write, 'We teach no new thing, but we repeat and establish old things, which the apostles and all godly teachers have taught before us.'[24] The English Reformers were equally clear. Hugh Latimer cried, 'But ye say, it is new learning. Now I tell you it is the old learning.'[25]

The same controversy over what is old and what is new continues to this day. The evangelical quarrel with anything that carries the label of a 'new reformation', a 'new theology', a 'new morality', even a 'new Christianity' is that it is, unfortunately, exactly what it says it is – new! It is not a valid reinterpretation of old first-century Christianity, for it deviates from this at many vital points. It is purely an invention of the modern age.

Evangelical believers, on the other hand, while recognizing the need to restate and reinterpret, are determined to remain loyal to the historic faith while doing so. What is needed is a translation of the gospel into the language, idiom and thought forms of the modern world. But it must be that – a genuine translation, not a fresh composition. What we are about is faithfully rendering something which has already been written or said into another language.

It is quite wrong, therefore, to accuse evangelicals of trying to introduce some new-fangled religion. Our whole aim is to recover primitive Christianity – the religion of the New Testament. The evangelist Billy Graham was once accused of 'putting the church back 50 years'. His response was to say, 'Of course, I'm disappointed in a way. I was trying to set it back a thousand years.' Or, better still, two thousand years!

4. Evangelical means fundamental

If 'evangelical' is a word describing a theology that is biblical and therefore 'original' in the sense of primitive, it also lays stress on what is fundamental. I hesitate to use this word, because the closely related term 'fundamentalist' has so many negative associations in our culture. In its original use, however, it had a much-needed emphasis, namely loyalty to what is 'fundamental' in biblical Christianity.

Christian fundamentalists are usually thought of as those who have an eccentric view of the Bible. They 'believe that every single word of the Bible is literally true', we are told, or something like this. It is true that evangelicals do believe in the divine origin and inspiration of the Bible (although they recognize that parts of it are intended to be figurative, and they do not believe that God 'dictated' it word for word to its human authors). But the doctrine of biblical authority is only one of several fundamental Christian doctrines which they believe – doctrines about God, Christ and the Holy Spirit, about sin and salvation, about the church and the sacraments, about worship, morality and evangelism, about death and the life to come.

It is because the fundamentals of the faith are at stake that evangelicals cannot afford to shy away from controversy and spend the rest of their days on some remote island of tranquillity and peace. No church or individual Christian can avoid the pain of debate and decision about these issues. To do so is to abandon the call to be responsible followers of Jesus Christ.

The evangelical insistence on fundamentals needs to be explained and qualified in two ways.

First, it does not mean that we expect all Christians to dot every 'i' and cross every 't' of our particular system. Our understanding of what is fundamental concerns what is plainly biblical. However, we recognize that the Bible does not speak on every issue with a clear and unmistakable voice. Matters such as how people should be baptized, the role of ordained ministry and styles of worship, cannot be regarded as fundamental. Indeed, any subject on which equally devout, equally humble, equally Bible-believing and Bible-studying Christians or churches reach different conclusions, must be considered secondary not primary. We must not insist on these as fundamentals but instead respect each other's integrity and acknowledge the legitimacy of each other's interpretations. The best guidance came from Rupert Meldenius at the beginning of the seventeenth century: 'In essentials unity, in non-essentials liberty, in all things love.'

The second qualification is this: in contending for the fundamentals of the faith, evangelical believers are not insisting on any particular way of expressing them. For example, it is a mistake to suppose that the only cry of evangelicals is 'back to the Reformation'. Greatly as we admire the godly scholarship and courage of the Reformers, and much as we thank God for his grace in and through them, we do not regard them with blind, unquestioning devotion. We do not believe in their infallibility. We only desire to go 'back to the Reformation' in the sense that we believe this to be the general theological position to which going 'back to the Bible' would take us. The same applies to all other systematizations of evangelical theology. Systematic theologies are of great value. But we know that biblical truth is greater than all attempts to systematize it.

In this connection evangelical Anglicans are fond of quoting some wise words of Charles Simeon. He was an evangelical minister in Cambridge at the beginning of the nineteenth

century who was a firm champion of evangelical truth despite
opposition which was fanatical at times. He lived in days when
the Calvinist–Arminian controversy raged fiercely, but he consistently refused to take sides. He stated his position by saying
that 'the truth is not in the middle, and not in one extreme, but
in both extremes . . . Sometimes I am a high Calvinist, at other
times a low Arminian, so that if extremes will please you, I am
your man; only remember, it is not one extreme that we are to
go to, but both extremes.'[26]

Charles Simeon warns us against choosing either one or other
extreme. Instead, his advice is to hold on to both extremes, as
long as they are equally biblical – even if our human minds
cannot reconcile or systematize them. For biblical truth is often
stated paradoxically. The attempt to resolve everything which
looks like a contradiction in the Bible's teaching is misguided
because it is impossible.

And so, when apparent opposites are encountered in the
Bible, 'it is possible that the truly scriptural statement will be
found, not in an exclusive adoption of either, nor yet in a
confused mixture of both, but in the proper and seasonable
application of them both.'[27]

This, then, is the claim which evangelical believers have
always made. It is that evangelical Christianity is theological in
its character, biblical in its substance, original in its history and
fundamental in its emphasis. My task in the rest of this book
is to set out some of its essential principles, as defended and
maintained by Jesus Christ himself.

CHAPTERS

1

Religion: Natural or supernatural?

The popular image of Christ as 'gentle Jesus, meek and mild' simply will not do. It is a false image. Certainly, he was full of love, compassion and tenderness. But he was also uninhibited when it came to exposing error and denouncing sin, especially hypocrisy. Christ was a controversialist. The Gospel writers show him as constantly debating with the religious leaders of his day. The purpose of studying his controversies is to make sure that the principles on which he took his stand are those which we are seeking to maintain today.

The first controversy we shall consider stems from a question which the Sadducees posed about the resurrection. It is strikingly relevant for today, because it highlights the issue of whether religion is natural or supernatural. Actually it goes further than this. It concerns not only what kind of religion the Christian religion is, but what kind of God the Christian God is. So it is fundamental.

The Sadducees and their modern counterparts

But before we listen to the Sadducees' question, we must take a look at the Sadducees themselves. They were a small but influential Jewish party, which had its origins in the days of the Maccabean dynasty, a century or so before Christ. Most of them lived in Jerusalem and were educated, wealthy and aristocratic. The high-priestly families were Sadducees, so that Luke is quite correct to identify 'the party of the Sadducees' with 'the high priest and all his associates'.[1] Although influential politically, they were unpopular because they collaborated with the authorities of the Roman occupation. Theologically they were conservative, accepting the written law (though in a very formal way) and rejecting the 'traditions of the elders' which were so much loved by the Pharisees. Thus, 'the Pharisees had an elaborate doctrine of immortality, resurrection, angels, demons, heaven, hell, the intermediate state and the Messianic kingdom, about all of which the Sadducees were agnostic.'[2] Flavius Josephus, the first-century Jewish historian, gave a succinct summary of this difference between the two major parties. The Pharisees, he wrote, 'believe that souls have an immortal vigour in them', whereas the Sadducees 'take away the belief of the immortal duration of the soul', teaching instead 'that souls die with the bodies'.[3]

This same basic theological distinction between the Pharisees and the Sadducees is faithfully recorded in the Gospels. Mark describes the Sadducees as those 'who say there is no resurrection'.[4] Similarly Luke comments in the Acts: 'The Sadducees say that there is no resurrection, and that there are neither angels nor spirits, but the Pharisees believe all these things.'[5]

We might therefore refer to the Sadducees as 'modernists'. Although in one sense theologically conservative, since they acknowledged the authority of the law of Moses, they were blind to the power of the living God which it reveals. They denied the supernatural.

Their contemporary equivalents are those who have absorbed the spirit of scientific materialism. Here are the kind of questions which modern Sadducees are asking: 'Hasn't science demonstrated that the universe is a closed, mechanistic system, and therefore done away with any need for God?' 'Isn't human experience to be explained entirely in terms of *natural* processes, so that we must reject even the possibility of the *super-natural*?' 'Isn't religion itself a natural phenomenon, having partly physiological and partly psychological causes, so that what it proves is not the existence of the God believed in but the disturbance in the brain chemistry of the believer?' 'And even if we can still believe in God as the creator and controller of the universe, surely we must now give up the old-fashioned idea that he has ever intervened *supernaturally* in human history, let alone that he still does so?'

These are typical questions asked by modern Sadducees. We discover how to answer them as we see how Jesus answered their ancient predecessors. These original Sadducees came to Jesus and began: 'Teacher, Moses wrote for us . . . '[6] We note that they referred to a passage in what we know as the Old Testament law of Moses (for which they held special respect) and that they regarded its message as having a contemporary application ('Moses wrote *for us* . . . '). The particular law to which they were referring laid down that a woman who was widowed and childless was not to be married 'outside the family to a stranger', but to her brother-in-law, her deceased husband's brother, so that he might 'build up his brother's house'. This was the background to the Sadducees' question. Here's how Mark sets it out:

Now there were seven brothers. The first one married and died without leaving any children. The second one married the widow, but he also died, leaving no child. It was the same with the third. In fact, none of the seven left any children. Last of all, the woman died too. At the resurrection [a resurrection, the Sadducees implied, in which the Pharisees believe, but we don't] whose wife will she be, since the seven were married to her?[7]

The Sadducees clearly thought they were being very clever and that by their imaginary case they had exposed what they saw as the absurdity of the doctrine of the resurrection. Their intention was to hold it up to ridicule. Their argument was that this life creates so many anomalies that to carry it on beyond the grave would be unthinkable. An afterlife would simply magnify the problems of this life. Take the poor woman in this question. She would be claimed by seven men, all seeking to be her husband. Would she have to reject them all (which would hardly be fair on her) or just choose one of them (which would be tough on the other six)? Or will she somehow be married to all seven at once? The Sadducees imagined that their problem had no solution. They thought they had caught Jesus out.

Jesus began and ended his reply with a clear statement of their error. 'You are in error,' he said (v. 24). 'You are badly mistaken' (v. 27). I have to say that I find his outspokenness very refreshing. Jesus did not compliment them, as we might have done, on getting hold of an important aspect of the truth, or on contributing a valuable insight to current theological debate. No. They were quite simply wrong.

He then added the reason for their mistake. They were wrong, he said, because they were ignorant. These educated aristocrats, priests and leaders of Israel, who believed in Moses' law and considered themselves extremely clever, were actually unaware of two truths: 'You do not know the Scriptures or the power of God' (v. 24). Their ignorance of Scripture was the immediate cause of their mistake about the resurrection, but the root cause was their ignorance of the power of God. We shall look at the causes of their error in this order (although Jesus discussed them in the opposite order). This means leaving verse 25 aside for the moment.

Ignorance of Scripture

We shall not go into this in any detail, because the supremacy of Scripture is the subject of the next chapter. But ignorance of Scripture is an issue here.

In general, Jesus traced the error of the Sadducees to their ignorance of the Bible. In the same way, most errors in the church today, especially those which lead to unnecessary controversy, are due to ignorance of or lack of respect for the Bible. It is highly significant that, in his disputes with both Pharisees and Sadducees, Jesus regarded Scripture as the authority in the debate and the final court of appeal. When they came to him with a question, he would usually respond with a counter-question which referred them to Scripture. For example, when a lawyer asked about eternal life, he replied, 'What is written in the law? How do you read it?'[8] Again, when the Pharisees enquired about his views on divorce, his immediate response was 'Have you not read?'[9] and 'What did Moses command you?'[10] It is the same here with the Sadducees. 'Have you not read in the book of Moses . . . ?' he asked. This was common ground between them. They had quoted Scripture; he quoted Scripture. They had referred to Moses; he also referred to Moses. In doing so, however, he had to draw attention to their misunderstanding, which was so great that it equated to ignorance.

In particular, he quoted Exodus 3:6, where, in the passage about the burning bush, God told Moses that he was 'the God of Abraham, the God of Isaac, and the God of Jacob'. This way

of describing himself, Jesus added, carried with it the implication of their resurrection, because 'He is not the God of the
dead, but of the living' (vv. 26, 27). The first point to note is
that the question at issue was not merely their survival, but their
resurrection. Christ introduced his answer with the words 'about
the dead rising' (v. 26). This is because, according to Scripture,
a human being is a combination of body and soul, whose final
destiny can't be fulfilled through the immortality of the soul
alone, but must also include the resurrection of the body.

Then there is a second point to consider. Is Christ's argument
fair? You might think that for God to call himself 'the God of
Abraham, Isaac and Jacob' implies no more than that he is the
God of history, the God who revealed himself successively to
the three generations of patriarchs.

But no. The words mean more than this, much more. The
argument rests not merely on the sentence 'I am the God of
Abraham, Isaac and Jacob', still less on the verb and its tense
'I am' (for in any case there is no verb in the Hebrew), but on
the whole context in which the sentence comes. The God who
is speaking is both the eternally *self-existing God* who reveals
himself as 'I am that I am' and the *covenant God* of Abraham,
Isaac and Jacob. He had made with Abraham 'an everlasting
covenant, to be your God and the God of your descendants
after you',[11] which he had then confirmed with Isaac and Jacob.
Further, his covenant promises were too extensive to be fulfilled
in their lifetime, and they knew it. According to the Epistle to
the Hebrews, 'they were foreigners and strangers on earth', who
'were longing for a better country – a heavenly one'.[12] So when
God announced himself to Moses as the God of Abraham, Isaac
and Jacob, he meant not only that he had been their God
centuries before, but that he was still their God and would be
to the end, keeping covenant with them, sustaining them with

his constant love. The God of ancient promise was the God of eternal fulfilment. 'He is not the God of the dead, but of the living; for,' as Luke adds, 'to him all are alive.'[13] The whole point of creating and choosing people was that they might live to him – and so it is ludicrous to suggest that God's purpose would be thwarted by death! The God of Abraham, Isaac and Jacob is himself the living God, and the living God is the God of the living.

This, then, was the first answer which Jesus gave to the Sadducees' question. They were ignorant of the Scriptures. As Luke's version puts it: 'even Moses showed that the dead rise.'[14] Yet for all their proud boast of loyalty to Moses, they had rejected what Moses himself said. Their minds had become blinded by prejudice or by rationalism or by the Greek culture they had absorbed. They no longer submitted to the revelation of God.

Ignorance of God's power

The more basic cause of the Sadducees' error, however, was their ignorance of the power of God.

They seem genuinely to have thought that their question about the law would be enough to overturn the notion of resurrection. In their opinion the problems which an afterlife would create made it unthinkable. They hoped that their story about the woman with seven husbands would lead to the idea being laughed out of court; we can almost hear their suppressed chuckles.

We are tempted instead, however, to laugh at how incredibly naïve they were. For underlying their argument was the wrong assumption that if there were another life beyond death and resurrection, then it would be *the same kind of life* as it had been before. It does not seem to have occurred to the Sadducees that

God could easily create another order of being, a new and different life in which earth's insoluble problems would be solved. They underestimated the power of God.

The Pharisees might well have been made uncomfortable by the Sadducees' question, for the Pharisees' notion of the next life was extremely materialistic. For example, 'the earth will assuredly restore the dead, which it now receives in order to preserve them, making no change in their form, but as it has received, so will it restore them.'[15] Hence 'posing resurrection riddles was a favourite game of the Sadducees and often an embarrassment to the Pharisees'.[16] But such questions would not embarrass Jesus, since he knew that the resurrection life would by the power of God be entirely different.

According to Luke, Jesus explained it like this: 'The people of this age marry and are given in marriage. But those who are considered worthy of taking part in the age to come and in the resurrection from the dead will neither marry nor be given in marriage, and they can no longer die; for they are like the angels. They are God's children, since they are children of the resurrection.'[17]

Here Jesus was following familiar Jewish thought and dividing history into two ages, present and future, 'this age' and 'the age to come'. He went on to emphasize that the life of the age to come will be significantly different from the life of this age. 'The people of this age marry and are given in marriage.' On the other hand, 'those who are considered worthy of taking part in the age to come and in the resurrection from the dead [none are worthy in themselves, but some by God's grace will be '*considered* worthy'] will neither marry nor be given in marriage.' Why not? Because 'they can no longer die'. How so? Because 'they are like the angels. They are God's children, since they are children of the resurrection.'

In other words, the new age will be populated by new beings living a new life under new conditions. Humans will be like angels. Mortals will have become immortal. To borrow a phrase from the apostle Paul, they will have been 'raised imperishable'.[18] Consequently, the need to propagate the human race will no longer exist. The creation command to 'be fruitful and increase in number; multiply on the earth and increase upon it'[19] will be cancelled. And in so far as reproduction is one of the chief purposes of marriage, humans will no longer marry. Not that love will cease, for 'love never ends'. But sexuality will be transcended, and personal relationships will be neither exclusive in their character nor physical in their expression.

And all this – this new life under new conditions in the new age – will be due to the power of God, of which the Sadducees were ignorant.

The contemporary debate
The Sadducees have many successors, who are equally clever and equally foolish. Some of them argue in almost identical terms. They caricature the resurrection in order to discredit it. They speak of it in grossly materialistic terms, as if 'resurrection' were the same as 'resuscitation'. They imagine that by the resurrection Christians mean the miraculous material reconstruction of the earthly body which will then continue as before. They go on to ask sceptically what happens to people whose bodies are blown to bits or whose ashes after cremation are scattered to the four winds. And they genuinely suppose that such questions will embarrass Christians and enable them to dismiss the doctrine of the resurrection as an absurdity! They have never grasped that the resurrection body, according to the New Testament, although retaining some continuity with the earthly body, will be altogether different, raised new and glorious by

the power of God. We can imagine the apostle Paul rebuking
them for their crude ideas in the same way that he scolded the
Corinthians who asked him, '*How* are the dead raised? With
what kind of body will they come?' 'How foolish!' Paul replied.
'When you sow, you do not plant the body that will be, but just
a seed, perhaps of wheat or of something else. But God gives
it a body as he has determined, and to each kind of seed he
gives its own body . . . So will it be with the resurrection of the
dead. The body that is sown is perishable, it is raised imperishable; it is sown in dishonour, it is raised in glory; it is sown in
weakness, it is raised in power; it is sown a natural body, it is
raised a spiritual body.'[20]

Other modern Sadducees are the scientific materialists whom
I mentioned earlier. Their view of reality is limited to what their
senses can grasp. They reject whatever cannot be scientifically
proved. They believe that the universe is a closed, self-explanatory
system, governed by so-called 'natural' laws. For them this has
two consequences.

First, they can find no room for God. In the early centuries
of the age of science, it was customary to distinguish between
natural law and divine action, the former being held to explain
what we can observe, while making some allowance for God in
those areas where no natural law could (yet) be discerned.
According to this viewpoint the great God of creation is thought
of as a mere 'God of the gaps'. One of the best examples of it
occurs in a letter which Isaac Newton wrote to the Master of
his College at Cambridge: 'the diurnal rotations of the planets
could not be derived from gravity, but required a divine arm to
impress it on them.'[21] In other words, 'natural law' (in this case
the law of gravity) is responsible for the orbiting of the earth
round the sun, but 'God' is responsible for its rotation on its
own axis. But this is asking for trouble. If God occupies only

the gaps, then as scientific discoveries increase and the gaps decrease, God is gradually edged out of his own universe.

But the Christian's God has never been a 'God of the gaps', however much some Christians have portrayed him as such. When the Marquis de Laplace 'was reproached by Napoleon for failing to mention God in his great treatise on celestial mechanics', he was right to reply, 'Sire, I have no need of that hypothesis.'[22] What he was denying by this statement was not God himself but the use of God as a plug to stop gaps with. For the same reason Bishop Samuel Wilberforce was wrong, in his debate with T. H. Huxley at a famous meeting of the British Association in Oxford in 1860, to describe Darwin's theory of evolution as 'an attempt to dethrone God'.[23] It does not necessarily aim to do any such thing, let alone succeed in the attempt. It is partly because Christians have often been misguided enough to defend some territory against the invasion of 'science' in order to preserve it for 'God' that the very notion of God has been dismissed by many scientists – like Julian Huxley, for example: 'The concept of God as a supernatural personal being is only a stop-gap explanation, advanced to stop the gaps in pre-scientific thought.'[24] Surely we must agree with Professor Donald MacKay that this 'dispute deserved to die, because it was not really between science and Christianity at all, but between mistaken views of each'.[25]

Then there is a second deduction which scientific materialists draw from their view of the universe as ruled by 'natural laws'. This is the denial of even the possibility of the 'supernatural'. 'Miracles *can't* happen,' they say. So 'miracles *don't* happen'. If they claim to be Christians at all, their 'Christianity' has been entirely drained of the miraculous.

How are we to reply to such critics as these, who first eliminate God from the natural and then proceed to get rid of the supernatural altogether? We must repeat Christ's own words: 'you are wrong because you do not know the power of God.'

To begin with, the God of the Bible is the God of nature, who himself has given and continues to give to nature its own consistent orderliness. The stop-gap theory of God was a convenient way of explaining the inexplicable. It drew an arbitrary distinction between what can and cannot (at the time of speaking) be rationally, scientifically explained, and then held onto God for the inexplicable and dismissed him from the explicable. If our concept of God is as mean as that, we deserve Julian Huxley's stinging rebuke: 'The god hypothesis is no longer of any pragmatic value for the interpretation or comprehension of nature, and indeed often stands in the way of better and truer interpretation. Operationally, God is beginning to resemble not a ruler but the last fading smile of a cosmic Cheshire Cat.'[26]

The truth is that no biblical Christian can accept the distinction between natural law and divine action which lies at the root of all this misunderstanding. For natural law is not an alternative to divine action, but a useful way of referring to it. So-called 'natural' laws simply describe a uniformity which scientists have observed. And Christians attribute this uniformity to the constancy of God. Further, to be able to explain a process scientifically is by no means to explain God away; it is rather (in the famous words of the German astronomer Johannes Kepler) to 'think God's thoughts after him' and to begin to understand his ways of working.

The Bible itself should have protected us from regarding God either as a stop-gap or as a machine-minder, for the God of the Bible dwells not in gaps but in all places, whether they appear to us to be full or empty. ' "Do I not fill heaven and earth?" declares the LORD.'[27] And the processes of nature are portrayed not as automatic mechanisms but as due to his own personal activity. Thus, God is said through Christ to be 'sustaining all things by his powerful word',[28] so that 'in him all things hold together'.[29] What is true of the whole universe is true of the planet on which we live. 'The earth is the Lord's, and everything in it';[30] and he has promised that 'As long as the earth endures, seedtime and harvest, cold and heat, summer and winter, day and night will never cease'.[31] Jesus himself could affirm in the Sermon on the Mount that it is God the Father who 'causes his sun to rise on the evil and the good, and sends rain on the righteous and the unrighteous'.[32] He is the God of history as well as of nature, supervising the migration of tribes and establishing the frontiers of nations. He 'gives everyone life and breath and everything else',[33] so that 'in him we live and move and have our being'.[34] He gives life to the lower creation also, feeds both animals and birds, and clothes the flowers of the field.

It's true that this is all pre-scientific – even naïve – language. It eliminates any second causes and explains the existence and continuation of all things, from the greatest to the least, as the direct activity of the living God. But it is still true. The scientific and the biblical ways of looking at nature do not contradict each other; they are complementary. Each explains something which the other does not explain. We must agree with Professor Charles Coulson: 'Either God is in the whole of Nature, with no gaps, or he's not there at all   If we cannot bring God in at the end of science, he must be there at the very start, and right through it. We have done wrong to set up any sharp antithesis between science and religion   There is no other way out of our impasse than to assert that science is one aspect of God's presence . . . '

Once we are clear about this, we shall know how to tackle today's Sadducees: 'It is on this issue that Christians will take exception to the scientific humanists,' comments Professor Coulson. 'This does not mean that they deny their science: but it does mean that they deplore their narrow-mindedness . . . A denial of God is practically always the result of shutting one eye. It may be for this reason that God gave us two.'

So the God revealed in the Bible is not a magician or wonder-worker, whose every act is a miracle. He normally works according to the natural order which he has himself established. At the same time, he is not imprisoned by nature or the laws of nature. It would be ridiculous to suppose that the creation now controls its Creator. He is able to step aside from his own uniformity, and the Bible says that he has sometimes done so. These miracles are not evenly spread throughout Scripture, but appear in clusters. Their clear purpose was to authenticate a fresh stage of God's self-disclosure to his chosen people. By specific, supernatural acts of salvation, revelation and judgment, he has made 'creative intrusions' into his own world.

Christianity a resurrection religion

Take resurrection, for example, as this was the point at issue with the Sadducees. The *natural* process which God has estab-lished, partly by creation and partly by judgment, is birth, growth, decay, death and decomposition. This is the cycle of nature. It includes human beings: 'for dust you are and to dust you will return.'[35] The very concept of 'resurrection' is therefore *supernatural*. At Christ's resurrection the natural process of physical decomposition was not only arrested, nor even reversed, but actually superseded. Instead of dissolving into dust, his body was transformed into a new and glorious vehicle for his soul. Indeed, the resurrection of Jesus is presented in the New Testament as the supreme manifestation of the super-natural power of God. Paul's prayer for the Ephesian Christians was that the eyes of their heart might be enlightened to know the incomparable greatness of God's power – the power which 'is the same as the mighty strength he exerted when he raised Christ from the dead . . . '[36]

Now Christianity is in its very essence a resurrection religion. The concept of resurrection lies at its heart. If you remove it, Christianity is destroyed. Let me show you what I mean.

The New Testament speaks of at least three separate resurrections.

First, *the resurrection of Christ.* About thirty-six hours after his death, his soul (which had been in Hades, the dwelling place of the dead) and his body (which had lain on a stone slab in his tomb) were reunited. At the same time his body was 'raised'. That is to say, it was transformed into what Paul calls 'his glorious body',[37] being invested with new and hitherto unknown powers. In this resurrection body Christ burst from the tomb, passed through closed doors, appeared to his disciples and disappeared, and finally, in defiance of the law of gravity, ascended out of sight.

Secondly, *the resurrection of the body.* The New Testament teaches that the resurrection of Jesus from the dead supplies both the proof and the pattern of the resurrection of our body on the last day. As he rose, so we shall rise – in fact and in manner. The apostle Paul is quite clear about it: 'Just as we have borne the image of the earthly man [i.e. Adam], so shall we bear the image of the heavenly man [i.e. Christ].'[38] And, when Christ returns, he 'will transform our lowly bodies so that they will be like his glorious body'. On that great day of Christ's return and our resurrection we shall be given bodies like his.

Thirdly, *the resurrection of sinners.* In affirming that Christianity is a resurrection religion, I do not mean that Christians simply look *back* 2,000 years to the resurrection of Jesus Christ and *forward* to the end when the general resurrection of the dead will take place. Between the past resurrection of

Christ and the future resurrection of the body another resurrection is taking place – the present and spiritual (though no
less supernatural) resurrection of sinners. Jesus himself talked
about receiving eternal life as a transition from death to life, a
resurrection of the dead: 'Very truly I tell you, whoever hears
my word and believes him who sent me has eternal life and will
not be judged but has crossed over from death to life. Very truly
I tell you, a time is coming and has now come when the dead
will hear the voice of the Son of God and those who hear will
live.'[39] The apostle Paul explained this further: 'As for you,
you were dead in your transgressions and sins . . . But because
of his great love for us, God, who is rich in mercy, made us
alive with Christ even when we were dead in transgressions – it
is by grace you have been saved. And God raised us up with
Christ and seated us with him in the heavenly realms in Christ
Jesus . . . '[40]

What exactly is this third resurrection? Is it a rather exaggerated and far-fetched description of what happens when people
turn over a new leaf? Indeed not. A resurrection by the power
of God is totally different from a reformation by the power of
human effort! What the gospel says is that the process called
'becoming a Christian' is actually a resurrection from the dead,
a deliverance from the spiritual grave to which our sin and guilt
had brought us. It is the gift of a new life, called 'eternal life', a
life lived in fellowship with God, so that Christians are those
who are 'alive from the dead'. It is being rescued from death,
raised to life, lifted up to heaven. It is a miracle, as divine and
supernatural an event as the resurrection of the body itself. It is
not *contrary* to nature but altogether *beyond* nature, since none
of us can raise ourselves from death or give ourselves a new life.
Once raised from spiritual death by God, the Christian lives in
newness of life. And so, having been 'raised with Christ', we are

told to 'set your hearts on things above, where Christ is, seated at the right hand of God'.[41]

These three resurrections are a vital part of the gospel which Paul preached. They can also be traced in the teaching of Jesus. 'The Son of man must . . . be killed,' he said, 'and on the third day be raised to life.'[42] In the same way every human being will rise on the last day. Indeed, 'that the dead are raised, even Moses showed'. And meanwhile, 'the Son gives life to whom he is pleased to give it',[43] reviving with eternal life those who are spiritually dead through sin.

Further, all three resurrections are miracles, supernatural events, and are down to the power of God. Thus it was God's 'incomparably great *power*'[44] which raised Christ from the dead. It is 'the *power* of Christ's resurrection'[45] which Paul said he wanted increasingly to experience and which is available to all who believe. And it will be the same divine '*power* that enables him to bring everything under his control' which, when Christ returns, 'will transform our lowly bodies so that they will be like his glorious body'.[46]

The church of Jesus Christ is today facing a major crisis of faith. At stake is nothing less than the essential character of the Christian religion: is it natural or supernatural? Various attempts have been made to rid Christianity of its supernaturalism, to reconstruct it without its embarrassing miracles. But these efforts are as unsuccessful as they are misguided. You cannot reconstruct something by first destroying it.

Authentic Christianity – the Christianity of Christ and his apostles – is supernatural Christianity. It is not a tame and harmless list of rights and wrongs, spiced with a dash of religion. It is rather a resurrection religion, a life lived by the power of God. The power that raised Christ from the dead and will one day raise us is able meanwhile to give us a new life, to transform who we are, what we do and how we do it.

The old dilemma between Jesus Christ and the Sadducees is still around today. 'There is no resurrection,' says the cynical modern Sadducee. To which Jesus Christ replies, 'You are greatly mistaken, because you know neither the Scriptures nor the power of God.'

2

Authority:
Tradition or Scripture?

We have seen that Jesus Christ was constantly engaged in controversy with the religious leaders of his day. They were critical of him and he was even more outspokenly critical of them. He did not hesitate when necessary to disagree with their views in public or to warn the people of their false teaching. 'Be on your guard against the yeast of the Pharisees and Sadducees,'[1] he said to his disciples. In the last chapter we considered his debate with the Sadducees about the character of religion; in this chapter we shall consider a debate he had with the Pharisees about the source of authority.

After the question of religion itself, which is about who God is and what he does, the next most vital question concerns authority. Whether we accept what anyone teaches depends on what we think of their authority. It is therefore perfectly understandable, and entirely justifiable, that the chief priests, elders and teachers of the law came to Jesus one day and asked him, 'By what authority are you doing these things, or who gave you this authority to do them?'[2] Christ's quarrel was with the insincerity that he detected behind their approach, not their actual question. Their question was right, even though their motives in asking it were wrong.

It's the same with Christianity today. Although all churches hold much belief in common, there are deep and wide differences. So how can we possibly know which church to believe and follow? It all comes down to the question of authority. What people are really asking is a whole series of questions like these: By what authority do you believe what you believe and teach what you teach? By what authority do you accept certain doctrines and reject others? And who gave you this authority? Is it a matter of opinion, of one person's conviction against another's or one church's confession against another's? Or is there an objective standard by which the teaching of all churches and Christians may be assessed and judged? Is there an independent judge to settle disputes? Is there any final and authoritative court of appeal?

From these general questions we move to the particular one which is of crucial importance. It is this. All churches assign some degree of authority to the Bible. But is Scripture the church's sole authority? Or may the church enhance the authority of Scripture with the authority of tradition? The word 'tradition' in a Christian context means simply the 'handing down' of Christianity from one generation to the next. If what had been handed down was just the Bible itself, then 'Scripture' would be the same as 'tradition' and there would be no problem about the relationship between them. But in fact – and rightly – each generation has also interpreted the faith and attempted to explain it, to apply it and then to hand it on. The result is that Scripture and tradition have become separated. This is why it has become necessary to ask what the relation is between them.

Although this is a live question today, it is not a modern problem. It was a bone of contention between the Pharisees and the Sadducees long ago. The first-century Roman-Jewish historian Josephus put it like this:

> What I would now explain is this, that the Pharisees have delivered to the people a great many observances by succession from their fathers, which are not written in the law of Moses; and for that reason it is that the Sadducees reject them, and say that we are to esteem those observances to be obligatory which are in the written word, but are not to observe what are derived from the tradition of our forefathers.[3]

The Pharisees' view of tradition

In the last chapter we saw Jesus take the side of the Pharisees against the Sadducees and demonstrate that religion is not natural but supernatural. In this chapter we shall watch him take the side of the Sadducees against the Pharisees and show that authority lies not in tradition but in Scripture. But he was not taking sides. For in both cases, though the company was different, his position was the same, namely an appeal to Scripture. He criticized the Sadducees for their ignorance of the Scriptures and attributed their error to this ignorance. He criticized the Pharisees because their traditions were making 'God's word null and void'.

We need now to look more closely at the comment of Josephus quoted above. The Pharisees clung tightly to a body of traditions they had inherited. They believed that these 'traditions of the fathers', although handed down orally and not found in the written law, had nevertheless been given to Moses on Mount Sinai in addition to the law. The Pharisees, therefore, thought that there were two parallel revelations from God, the written law and the oral tradition, both equally important and equally authoritative.

During the second century BC these oral traditions came to be preserved in written form in what is known as the Mishnah. It has six divisions containing laws about agriculture, festivals and marriage, together with civil, criminal and ceremonial laws. It was supplemented later by the Gemara, which is a commentary on it. The Mishnah and the Gemara together form the Jewish Talmud.

Several quotations could be given to illustrate the devotion and reverence which the Jews felt for this collection of tradition. In one of the Rabbinic Targums (which are Aramaic paraphrases of the Old Testament) God is even represented as 'busying himself by day with the study of the Scriptures, and by night with that of the Mishnah'.[4] At a later period the rabbis would say, 'The Scriptures are water; the Mishnah, wine; but the Gemara, spiced wine.'[5]

If the tendency of the Sadducees was to undermine the authority of the Scriptures by their superficial interpretations, the Pharisees tended to smother the Scriptures with a mass of traditions. Put simply, the Pharisees *added* to the Word of God, while the Sadducees *subtracted* from it. Both practices are equally wrong and dangerous.

We turn now to the details of Christ's controversy with the Pharisees over authority, as recorded by Mark:

> The Pharisees and some of the teachers of the law who had come from Jerusalem gathered around Jesus and saw some of his disciples eating food with hands that were defiled, that is, unwashed. (The Pharisees and all the Jews do not eat unless they give their hands a ceremonial washing, holding to the tradition of the elders. When they come from the market-place they do not eat unless they wash.

And they observe many other traditions, such as the washing of cups, pitchers and kettles.)

So the Pharisees and teachers of the law asked Jesus, 'Why don't your disciples live according to the tradition of the elders instead of eating their food with defiled hands?'

He replied, 'Isaiah was right when he prophesied about you hypocrites; as it is written:

"These people honour me with their lips,
    but their hearts are far from me.
They worship me in vain;
    their teachings are merely human rules."

You have let go of the commands of God and are holding on to human traditions.'

And he continued, 'You have a fine way of setting aside the commands of God in order to observe your own traditions! For Moses said, "Honour your father and mother," and, "Anyone who curses their father or mother is to be put to death." But you say that if anyone declares that what might have been used to help their father or mother is Corban (that is, devoted to God) – then you no longer let them do anything for their father or mother. Thus you nullify the word of God by your tradition that you have handed down. And you do many things like that.'[6]

The cause of this public controversy was that the Pharisees saw some of the disciples of Jesus eating food with hands 'defiled' (v. 2). The Greek adjective *koinos* means 'common', i.e. 'ritually unclean'. Mark adds his own editorial comment that the disciples' hands were 'unwashed'. We need to understand that the issue was not one of medical hygiene, but of ceremonial purification. In a lengthy explanation in verses 3 and 4 Mark gives his Gentile readers a more elaborate explanation. 'The Pharisees, and all the Jews' (because these Pharisaic principles were popular), he writes, 'do not eat unless they give their hands a ceremonial washing, holding to the tradition of the elders.' Especially 'when they come from the market-place,' he adds, where they might contract all sorts of defilement and where the disciples may themselves just have been, 'they do not eat unless they wash.' It doesn't stop there. There are many other traditions which they observe, such as the ceremonial 'washing of cups, pitchers and kettles'.

So the Pharisees came to Jesus and said, 'Why don't your disciples live according to the tradition of the elders instead of eating their food with defiled hands?' (v. 5). We are going to examine carefully how Jesus replies. To begin with, he had something to say about their views on purification, and applied to them a word of God spoken through Isaiah to Israel: 'These people honour me with their lips, but their hearts are far from me. They worship me in vain . . . ' The vanity of their worship is that it was all on the outside. It was merely an affair of the lips, not the heart. We shall consider this more fully in later chapters about the essential inwardness of Christian morality and worship.

Jesus then went on to say something about their view of tradition. In opposition to the opinions of the Pharisees, he set out three important principles. First, that Scripture is divine, while tradition is human. Secondly, that Scripture is compulsory, while tradition is optional. Thirdly, that Scripture is supreme, while tradition is secondary. We will consider these principles in turn.

Scripture divine, tradition human

What does Jesus say about tradition? The Pharisees referred to it as 'the tradition of the elders' (vv. 3, 5). But Jesus called what they were so keen on merely 'human rules' (v. 7) and 'human traditions' (v. 8).

Now this immediately cut the ground from under the Pharisees' feet. As we have already seen, they believed that Scripture and tradition were equally ancient, equally from Moses, equally divine. Christ did not share this view. On the contrary, he drew a sharp distinction between the two. On the one hand there was what '*Moses* said' (v. 10), and on the other what '*you* say' (v. 11). At first sight one might think that this was simply to set two Jewish teachers or schools of thought, Moses and the elders, in opposition to each other. But this is not at all how Jesus saw the disagreement. To him Moses and the elders were not at all similar, for the elders were fallible men with human traditions, while Moses was God's spokesman. So what '*you* say' is equivalent to '*your* tradition' (vv. 9, 13) or 'the *human* traditions' (v. 8), whereas what '*Moses* said' are 'the commands of *God*' (vv. 8, 9) and 'the word of *God*' (v. 13). To put this beyond doubt we notice that the phrase '*Moses* said' in verse 10 is rendered in Matthew 15:4 '*God* said', and that this was the consistent approach taken by Jesus and his apostles. For them, 'Scripture says' and 'God says' meant the same.

Here then we have our Lord's own authority for saying that the distinction between Scripture and tradition is the same as the distinction between God's Word written and all human interpretations and additions.

Put another way, we may say that the only 'tradition' that Scripture recognizes is Scripture itself. For 'tradition' is what is handed down, and God's purpose has been that his Word, his unique revelation given to prophets and apostles, should be transmitted from generation to generation. So the apostle Paul wrote to Timothy, 'The things you have heard me say in the presence of many witnesses entrust to reliable people who will also be qualified to teach others.'[7] From Paul to Timothy, from Timothy to reliable people, and from them to others also. *This* is the true apostolic succession; it is the transmission of apostolic doctrine. By this written apostolic tradition the early church learned to judge all teaching, subjecting it to the test which Paul himself had commanded, namely whether it was 'according to the teaching you received from us' (i.e. from the apostles).[8] As Dean Henry Alford put it when commenting on 2 Timothy 2:2, 'Scripture has been God's way of fixing tradition, and rendering it trustworthy at any distance of time.'[9]

Just as Jesus distinguished between Moses and the elders, so we must distinguish between *apostolic* tradition (which is Scripture) and *ecclesiastical* tradition (which is the teaching of the church). We must also say with him that the latter is human, but the former divine.

Scripture compulsory, tradition optional

While we seek to follow Christ in making a clear distinction between Scripture and tradition, we must be careful not to overstate the case. Jesus did not reject all human traditions out of hand, forbidding his disciples to cherish or follow any of them. What he did was to put tradition in its place, namely a secondary place, and then, provided that it was not contrary to Scripture, to make it optional.

This is what the Pharisees were failing to do. According to the second part of the quotation from Isaiah, 'their teachings are merely human rules'. The word used for 'teachings' here is *didaskalia*, which means 'a definite piece or course of instruction'.[10] In other words, the Pharisees were taking their own inherited but human rules and presenting them as authoritative teaching. They were trying to make others go beyond what God had commanded. In doing this they were exalting their tradition into a position of authority equivalent to the revealed commands of God, which was practically the same as saying that the observance of their traditions was necessary to salvation. But this is not so.

Take the purification rituals of the Pharisees. There is nothing wrong with cleaning the vessels from which food is to be served or in washing our hands before eating it. Hygienically, it is a very sensible thing to do. Ceremonially, it is a pretty harmless one. It is certainly not against Scripture. But at the same time, it is not commanded by God in his Word, and so the Pharisees had no right to elevate it to the status of a divine requirement and make it compulsory.

Their regulations about 'Corban' were similar. This had to do with the keeping of vows, which the law was clear in saying should be kept. But the Pharisees went beyond Scripture and laid down detailed rules so that, in certain situations, Jesus had to say to them, 'you no longer let' a person follow a certain course (v. 12). This is a very revealing expression. It indicates that the Pharisees were setting themselves up as moral judges, commanding certain practices and prohibiting others. They were giving and withholding permission in matters in which God had given them no right to interfere.

So Jesus insisted that those harmless traditions, which are neither required nor forbidden by Scripture, must be regarded as optional. Because they are merely 'human rules' they may never be made compulsory. People are free with regard to them. The fact that Jesus neither justified nor rebuked his disciples' breach of the Pharisees' ritual traditions tells us that he was quite relaxed about them. What he resisted and condemned was any attempt to impose traditions as being essential.

This is the doctrine of the sufficiency of Scripture, which the sixteenth-century Reformers understood very well. The Church of England expresses the matter clearly in her Articles of Religion. Article VI reads: 'Holy Scripture containeth all things necessary to salvation: so that whatsoever is not read therein, nor may be proved thereby, is not to be required of any man, that it should be believed as an article of the Faith, or be thought requisite or necessary to salvation.'

This does not mean that the church has no authority. Harmless traditions not contrary to Scripture are permissible, but they may not be made mandatory. Article XX reads: 'The Church hath power to decree Rites or Ceremonies . . . And yet it is not lawful for the Church to ordain any thing that is contrary to God's Word written . . . Wherefore, although the Church be a witness and a keeper of holy Writ, yet, as it ought not to decree anything against the same, so besides the same ought it not to enforce any thing to be believed for necessity of Salvation.' The distinction is clear. The church never has the authority to decree anything 'against' Scripture. 'Besides' (i.e. in addition to) Scripture it may make rules, but only as long as it does not make them a condition of salvation.

Let me illustrate the principle from the practice of the Church of England. It is traditional in the Church of England for candidates for baptism to be signed with the sign of the cross on their forehead, as an indication that they will 'not be ashamed to confess the faith of Christ crucified'. Other traditions include the practice of the bride (and often the groom as well) receiving a ring during the marriage ceremony; for the coffin to be brought into church during the funeral service; and for ministers to wear certain robes during public worship. None of these customs is commanded in Scripture. At the same time, they are not contrary to Scripture. Therefore they are permissible, provided that they are not given divine authority or enforced upon people as essential to salvation.

What is true of churches is equally true of individual Christians. We may value certain traditions, either in what we believe or in what we do. For example, we may have adopted particular ways of approaching prayer, Bible reading, attendance at Holy Communion, fasting, or Christian giving. Provided that our choices in these areas are not contrary to the Bible's teaching, we are free to practise them. But we have no right to attempt to force our ways of doing things on others. To do so is to elevate merely human rules to a status they do not deserve. Other people must have the freedom to reject them.

Scripture supreme, tradition secondary

The third principle which Jesus set out, namely regarding the supremacy of Scripture, he developed from the teaching of the Pharisees about Corban.

'Corban' means a gift or offering which is consecrated to God. When something was set aside as 'Corban', however, it was not necessarily given to God then and there. The idea was to identify things that would be given to God at some time in the future. From this developed the tradition that something labelled as 'Corban' could not later be diverted to any other purpose. Furthermore, when the word 'Corban' was used in a formula of making a vow, the vow was regarded as absolutely binding. Indeed, the Pharisees went so far as to say that such a vow was binding, even if what was vowed involved breaking the law!

Now the case presented in this controversy of Christ with the Pharisees is of a young man who, either piously or rashly, has taken a vow about his money. He has designated it as 'Corban' and therefore (according to the tradition) has prevented it from being used for anything else, even the support of his parents in their old age. To Jesus, however, this was quite wrong. As far as he was concerned, the issue was simple. Moses had settled it by a clear command and warning (v. 10). The command was 'Honour your father and mother,'[11] and the warning 'Anyone who curses their father or mother [how much more he who *does* evil to them?] is to be put to death.'[12]

'*But you*,' Jesus continues, emphasizing the contrast between the teaching of the Pharisees and the teaching of Moses, 'you say that if anyone declares that what might have been used to help their father or mother is Corban (that is, devoted to God)' then he need not 'do anything for their father or mother. Thus you nullify the word of God by your tradition that you have handed down.' Furthermore, 'you do many things like that' (vv. 11–13). That is, the same principle of cancelling out Scripture by tradition comes again and again in what you do.

It may be helpful at this point to state Christ's second and third principles side by side. The second is that traditions which are not in conflict with Scripture (like the washing of hands and vessels) are permissible if optional. The third principle is that traditions which are in conflict with Scripture (like the Corban vow which led to the dishonouring of a person's parents) must be firmly rejected. The point is that Scripture is always supreme, and tradition must always be secondary.

In order to put it beyond doubt, Jesus repeats this third principle three times. Verse 8: 'You have let go of the commands of God and are holding on to human traditions.' Verse 9: 'You have a fine way of setting aside the commands of God in order to observe your own traditions!' Verse 13: 'Thus you nullify the word of God by your tradition that you have handed down.' In each case Jesus sets human traditions and the commandments of God in opposition, and forbids us to 'let go', 'set aside' or 'nullify' God's Word in order to 'hold onto' or 'observe' our tradition. In fact, we should do the exact opposite. Our duty is to 'hold onto' or 'observe' God's Word, and if necessary 'let go' and 'set aside' our traditions in order to do so. This is even clearer in Matthew's version of this incident, where the key concept is that of 'breaking' a law or rule. The Pharisees asked, 'Why do your disciples *break* the tradition of the elders?' Jesus replied, 'And why do you *break* the command of God for the sake of your tradition?'[13]

The error of the Pharisees should now be clear. It's true that this was not their intention. They claimed that the oral tradition was a 'fence for Torah' – that is to say, a protective barrier to preserve the integrity of the law – 'but in actual fact it tampered with the Law'.[14] Further, in practice they seem to have preferred their own traditions, with one of them (Rabbi Jochanan) going so far as to say that 'the words of the teachers of the law are loved more than the words of the law'.[15]

Jesus was firmly opposed to this. When Scripture and tradition are in collision, he insisted, Scripture is supreme over tradition. God's Word about the honour due to parents must take precedence over human tradition about Corban vows. This was a principle which Jesus expressed and applied on many occasions. His reverent acceptance of the divine origin and supreme authority of the Old Testament Scriptures is beyond question. In the Sermon on the Mount, for example, and in his teaching about Sabbath observance and divorce, he went back behind accumulated tradition and appealed directly to God's written Word. To him Scripture was always the final court of appeal. 'Have you not read?' he would ask. 'What is written in the law?' What is written and may be read, i.e. the teaching of Scripture, must be what settles every dispute.

We are now able to put together the three principles which Jesus set out in this debate with the Pharisees. He taught the divinity, the sufficiency and the supremacy of Scripture. He affirmed that Scripture does not need to be supplemented by any binding traditions, and that it is the supreme authority by which all traditions must be judged. The foundation on which he built these two truths is the divine origin and inspiration of Scripture. Tradition is the word of human beings, but Scripture is the Word of God.

We turn now from the principles we find in the Bible to how they have applied in history.

The Reformers and the supremacy of Scripture

The relation between Scripture and tradition was one of the principal issues of the Reformation. Both sides accepted the divine inspiration and authority of the Bible. They did not disagree about this. The issue was whether Scripture had *sole* authority, whether its teaching was sufficient for salvation without any unbiblical additions, and whether it was supreme over even the most ancient traditions of the church.

Rome said 'No'. Like the Pharisees, she relied much on what she termed 'unwritten traditions'. Indeed, there is great similarity between the Roman and the Pharisaic views of tradition. Both Pharisees and Roman Catholics believed their tradition to be as inspired as Scripture. The Pharisees traced theirs back to Moses, while the Roman Catholics traced theirs to Christ. Thus, a rabbi could declare in the Mishnah: 'Moses received the (oral) Law from Sinai, and delivered it to Joshua and Joshua to the elders, and the elders to the prophets and the prophets to the men of the great synagogue.' Similarly, Rome asserted that her traditions had been 'received by the Apostles from the mouth of Christ himself, or from the Apostles themselves, the Holy Ghost dictating'.[16] The Fourth Session of the Council of Trent in 1546 had this to say: 'Scripture and tradition are to be received by the Church as of equal authority.' Again, the Council 'receives and venerates with equal affection of piety and reverence' both Scripture and tradition. Consequently the Church of Rome did not reform herself according to Scripture or purge out of her system those traditions about (for example) the Virgin Mary, the Mass, the priesthood, purgatory and indulgences which had grown up over the centuries but which Scripture either did not teach or actively contradicted.

The Reformers thought differently. *Sola Scriptura*, by Scripture alone, was one of the rocks on which they built. They knew that the early church had had good reason to decide what belonged in the New Testament, i.e. to fix and close the canon of the New Testament. This wasn't a matter of the church exercising authority over the biblical books, but simply acknowledging the authority they already had. This showed that there was a clear line to be drawn between apostolic tradition and ecclesiastical tradition, and that the apostolic traditions of the New Testament books were the 'canon', the standard or measuring rule, by which the traditions of the church must always be tested. They also knew that the early church Fathers understood this. 'All contention which the old fathers had with heretics was for the Scriptures,' wrote Cranmer, ' . . . but for things which are not contained in the Scriptures they never accused any man of heresy.'[17] In other words, Scripture was their rule.

This same issue between Scripture and tradition was highlighted by the Reformer Hugh Latimer in his 'Sermon of the Plough', preached outside St Paul's Cathedral on 18 January 1548. In it he described the devil as 'the most diligent bishop and prelate in all England', who is 'never out of his diocese' but is 'the diligentest preacher in all the realm'. And where the devil is resident, Latimer continued, 'and hath his plough going', 'there away with books and up with candles, away with Bibles and up with beads . . . up with man's traditions and his laws, down with God's tradition and his most holy word'.[18]

The reformed Church of England teaches clearly in its Articles both the sufficiency and the supremacy of Scripture. It does so not only in the plain statements of Articles VI and XX already quoted, but by the frequent biblical allusions and applications of these two principles throughout. Again and again they affirm the acceptance of one doctrine because it 'may be proved by most certain warrants of holy Scripture', and equally the rejection of another because it is 'a fond [i.e. foolish] thing vainly invented, and grounded upon no warranty of Scripture, but rather repugnant to the Word of God'.

The reformed Church of Scotland also clearly teaches the same thing: 'The whole counsel of God, concerning all things necessary for his own glory, man's salvation, faith, and life, is either expressly set down in scripture, or by good and necessary consequence may be deduced from scripture: unto which nothing at any time is to be added, whether by new revelations of the Spirit, or traditions of men.'[19]

Not only is Scripture (in all essential matters) sufficient of itself without supplementary traditions; it is also the means by which the truth and value of all traditions are to be assessed: 'The supreme Judge, by which all controversies of religion are to be determined, and all decrees of councils, opinions of ancient writers, doctrines of men, and private spirits, are to be examined, and in whose sentence we are to rest, can be no other but the Holy Spirit speaking in the scripture.'

Some practical conclusions

So far we have concentrated on principles drawn from the Bible (as set out by Jesus in controversy with the Pharisees) and examples taken from history. But our discussion needs to be earthed in the reality of today. So let me make three suggestions about the place of tradition.

First, we must distinguish more clearly between tradition and
Scripture. Many Christians have a set of cherished beliefs
and practices, perhaps inherited from their parents or learned
in childhood from the church. Too many of us have taken them
on board without thinking them through. Evangelical believers
are by no means free of this tendency. For example, take the
suggestion that young Christians should avoid going to night
clubs. I am not expressing an opinion on whether this particular
activity is right or wrong. All I want to point out is that Scripture
contains no explicit pronouncement about it. A prohibition like
this belongs therefore to 'the traditions of the evangelical elders';
it is not part of the Word of God. No Christian can escape the
responsibility of trying to think biblically and to decide carefully
about questions like this. We have the freedom to make up our
own minds. And that means that we have no right to make up
other people's minds for them or to stand in judgment on others
if they disagree with us. We need to say to ourselves again and
again, as Christ taught the Pharisees, that 'Scripture is compulsory, but tradition optional'.

Secondly, we must value tradition for what it is, rather than
for what it is not. In their concern to assert the supremacy of
Scripture, evangelicals have often been scornful of tradition.
But we should not despise or reject all tradition unthinkingly.
Some traditions are the church's ways of expressing thoroughly
biblical truth, such as the creeds and confessions of the Christian
Faith. And very valuable they are too. Indeed, we believe that
the Holy Spirit himself has guided this historical development
of tradition. Professor James Orr argued in his book *The Progress
of Dogma*[20] that, as the church clarified its thinking down the
centuries, the chronological order in which doctrines were
worked out was the logical order. Starting with what Christians
believe about God himself, we can trace how the church's

understanding developed as it moved on to the relationships between the three Persons of the Trinity and between the two natures of Christ, and then to the great doctrines of humanity, sin, grace, the atonement and salvation. Is it not right to trace the hand of the Holy Spirit in this unfolding process? One reason for rejecting the outlook which wants to replace our allegedly 'outworn' ancient blueprints with something new is precisely that it shows so little respect for the development of theology throughout history and therefore for the work of the Holy Spirit. Having said this, however, we must emphasize that even our most hallowed historical traditions are not the same as Scripture. Although the Holy Spirit has been active both in the work of revelation (through the authors of Scripture) and in illumination (through the interpreters of Scripture), these two must be distinguished. The church's creeds and confessions are not infallible. They must be weighed and maybe even amended as the Holy Spirit causes further light to break upon us from the Bible. The only unalterable expressions of truth are those we find in the pages of Scripture.

Thirdly, we must be rigorous in submitting tradition to Scripture. This applies to both churches and individuals.

Every church should engage in continuous self-reformation, examining its traditions in the light of Scripture and where necessary changing them. This is particularly true in the case of churches who decide to unite. Evangelicals hold different views regarding the nature of Christian unity and whether the drawing of churches together is a desirable goal. But all would agree that no movement towards reunion can be pleasing to God or good for the church unless it is at the same time a movement towards reformation. True unity will always be unity in truth, and truth means biblical truth. If only church leaders would sit down with their Bibles, would make clear distinctions between apostolic traditions (which are biblical) and ecclesiastical traditions (which are not), and would agree to submit the latter to the former by requiring the former of each other but giving each other freedom over the latter, immediate and solid progress could be made.

In recent decades, one of the great obstacles in schemes for bringing about union between churches has been the so-called 'historic episcopate', that is to say, the need to have bishops who are in historic succession from the apostles. Quite apart from the question whether such an episcopate is indeed 'historic' (either in origin or in unbroken continuity), it is certainly a non-biblical tradition. *Episkopē* (the Greek word for pastoral oversight) is required by Scripture, and is described there as a gift of God to his church; but the particular patterns of episcopal ministry we find in the church today are not. Churches are right, therefore, to insist on the former but not the latter.

Anglican evangelicals may regard the historic episcopate as an acceptably biblical form of *episkopē* (though it has by no means always been in line with the scriptural ideals of pastoral oversight). They may also value it as a symbol of continuity and a focus of unity in the church. But to acknowledge its potential value in their own church is one thing; to insist upon it as a condition of union with other churches is something quite different. Those who do this are not only hindering the church's progress towards unity, but also going against a principle laid down by the church's Lord. They are insisting on sticking with rules that are merely human. They are failing to submit tradition to Scripture.

It is easy to point an accusing finger at others. But let's not forget that the need to submit tradition to Scripture applies not just to churches but also to individual Christians. We urgently need to study the Scripture with greater care and humility, with a view to submitting our whole mind, will and life to what God has said in his Word.

3

The Bible: End or means?

Jesus had two controversies with the Jews about the Bible. The first, which we considered in the last chapter, was about its nature as God's written Word, and what follows from this about its supremacy over human traditions and its sufficiency for salvation without them. His second controversy, to which we turn our attention in this chapter, was concerned principally with its function, the reason God had given it to his people.

Jesus Christ gave Scripture a very exalted position. He clearly asserted its divine origin and authority. But he also warned us of the possibility of over-exalting it (as the Jews were doing) by making it an end in itself. The God-given purpose of Scripture is to point and lead people to Christ. It was never intended as an end in itself, but as a means to that end.

This further controversy of Christ (about the true function of Scripture) is relevant to the theological debates of our day too. As we have seen, many people have too 'low' a view of Scripture; they do not accept it (as Jesus did) as the written Word of God. At the same time, there are others whose view of

Scripture is too 'high'. They regard Scripture with an almost superstitious reverence. They become so absorbed in Scripture itself that they lose sight of its purpose, which is to reveal Christ to them. They end up being, in effect, 'bibliolaters' or 'Bible-worshippers', behaving as if Scripture rather than Christ were the object of their devotion.

Now evangelicals have, or should have, an extremely high view of the divine inspiration of Scripture (a view as high as Christ's own view, in fact). But we must be careful not to be open to the charge of bibliolatry and, if we find ourselves accused of this, we must be able to respond. We must show clearly in our attitudes and in our behaviour that our ultimate pre-occupation is not with Scripture itself, but with the Christ to whom Scripture points us.

This is how Jesus criticized his contemporaries: 'You study the Scriptures diligently because you think that in them you have eternal life. These are the very Scriptures that testify about me, yet you refuse to come to me to have life.'[1]

In these verses Jesus gave a concise summary of both the divine origin and the practical purpose of Scripture.

Scripture's divine origin

'It is they that testify about me,' he said. In saying this, he implied that their origin is divine.

In order to appreciate the force of this, we need to see it in its context. Most of John 5 is taken up with why we should put our faith in Christ. The chapter begins on a Sabbath day in Jerusalem, beside the Sheep Gate pool called Bethesda. Here Jesus healed an invalid who had been ill for thirty-eight years. 'Get up,' he said to him, 'pick up your mat and walk.' The Jews immediately raised objections. First, they told the man off for unlawfully carrying his mat on the Sabbath (v. 10).

Then they rebuked Jesus for unlawfully healing him on the Sabbath (v. 16).

In the discussion that follows, Jesus enlarged on his claim to be working together with his Father (v. 17). The divine work which he was doing was twofold – giving life to the dead (v. 21) and judging (v. 22). Everyone who hears and believes, he declared, receives eternal life there and then, and will escape judgment; he has already crossed over from death into life (v. 24).

Having made this astonishing claim, Jesus went on to repeat it still more forcefully. The dead were already hearing his voice, he maintained, and those who were hearing were receiving life and coming out of their spiritual graves (v. 25). That is, a sifting process was going on, because the Father had given to the Son both to have life in himself and authority to carry out judgment (vv. 26, 27). More than that, on the last day, all in their graves ('all' is emphatic here) would hear his voice and come out. Then the sifting of judgment would be brought to completion, for some would 'rise to live', while others would 'rise to be condemned' (vv. 28, 29).

This twofold claim of Jesus (to have the authority to bring to life and to carry out judgment) had tremendous implications, which the Jews were not slow to grasp. It comes as no surprise that they tried to kill him for what they took to be blasphemy (v. 18). For life-giving and judging are both things that only God can do. Yet Jesus dared to say that they had been given over to him. He was already bringing some to life and judging others, he said; and on the last day his work as Life-giver and Judge would reach its completion.

But how could people believe his claims? This is the question that Jesus now deals with. He begins by clearing himself of all self-importance. He is acting not on his own authority, but on God's, he says. Nor is he seeking his own will, but God's (v. 30).

In the same way (v. 31) he does not rely on his own testimony (for nobody can be a witness in his own case), but on God's. Verse 32: 'There is another who testifies in my favour, and I know that his testimony about me is true.' This 'another' is God the Father. It's true that there were other human witnesses and still are. There was John the Baptist (v. 32), 'a lamp that burned and gave light' (v. 35). There was John the writer of this Fourth Gospel also, whose whole book is a testimony to Christ. But the claims of Jesus were so far-reaching that he needed testimony which was stronger than that which mere human beings could offer. He needed testimony from God.

And this is what he claimed to have. 'Not that I accept human testimony . . . I have testimony weightier than that of John . . . the Father who sent me has himself testified concerning me' (vv. 34, 36, 37).

What, then, is the Father's testimony to the Son? What form has this divine witness taken? Jesus explains that it is a twofold testimony – in works and in words. First, in works, the things Jesus did. 'For the works that the Father has given me to finish – the very works that I am doing – testify that the Father has sent me' (v. 36; cf. 14:10, 11). So the mighty works of Jesus, because they were done by the Father's power, were the first part of the Father's witness to him. But the Father's testimony takes a second form too. 'And the Father who sent me has himself testified concerning me' (v. 37), not now indirectly through the works he has enabled Jesus to do, but in some way directly, 'himself'. Further, he 'has testified concerning me' (a perfect tense), which implies that it is a witness from the past which continues to be valid in the present. How? Not in voice ('you have never heard his voice'), nor in vision ('nor seen his form'), but in a written word which could be received but, sad to say, 'nor does his word dwell in you'. This is clear because 'you do not believe the one he sent' (vv. 37, 38). 'You study the Scriptures diligently . . . the very Scriptures that testify about me, yet you refuse to come to me' (vv. 39, 40). Jesus identifies the Scriptures as the Father's word which does not dwell in them, the Father's testimony which they have read but rejected.

Christ's view of Scripture
Looking back over this chapter which we have examined, the sequence of thought is plain. Jesus was making great claims when he said he had authority to bring to life and to judge, for these are activities of God. When challenged, he said he had testimony enough to back up his claims, neither self-testimony, nor human testimony, but divine. And this divine testimony consisted partly of the mighty works which the Father had given him to do, but especially of the written word of Scripture.

This, then, was Jesus Christ's view of the Scriptures. Their witness is God's witness. The testimony of the Bible is the testimony of God. And this is the chief reason why the Christian believes in the divine origin of the Bible – the fact that Jesus Christ himself taught it.

Moreover, he taught it consistently. He adopted towards the Scriptures of the Old Testament an attitude of reverent assent and submission, and he maintained this position throughout his life and ministry, including the post-resurrection period. According to John, he said, 'Scripture cannot be set aside'[2] and, according to Matthew, 'not the smallest letter, not the least stroke of a pen, will by any means disappear from the Law until everything is accomplished.'[3] He accepted the statements of Scripture without question, believing them to be true. He confidently predicted his rejection by his own people, his sufferings, death and resurrection, because this was what was written about him. He obeyed the requirements and applied the principles of

Scripture in his everyday life. He voluntarily accepted a position of humble submission to what Scripture said. The word *gegraptai* ('it stands written') was enough to settle any issue for him.[4] He understood his mission in the light of Old Testament prophecy, recognizing and declaring himself to be both Daniel's Son of man[5] and Isaiah's suffering Servant of the Lord.[6] At least from the age of twelve he felt the compulsion of Scripture upon his soul, an inner constraint to fulfil the role which Scripture set out for him. Thus, 'Didn't you know I had to be in my Father's house?'[7] 'He then began to teach them that the Son of Man must suffer many things and be rejected . . . and that he must be killed and after three days rise again.'[8] 'The Son of man goes as it is written of him.'[9] 'We are going up to Jerusalem, and everything that is written by the prophets about the Son of Man will be fulfilled.'[10] No wonder the apostle Paul could later write that 'he humbled himself by becoming obedient to death'.[11] When Peter tried to prevent his arrest in the garden, Jesus rebuked him: 'Do you think I cannot call on my Father, and he will at once put at my disposal more than twelve legions of angels? But how then would the Scriptures be fulfilled that say it must happen in this way?'[12]

Furthermore, he also expected others to believe and practise what he himself believed and practised with regard to the authority of Scripture. In debate with religious leaders, as we have seen, it was obvious to him that Scripture must be the court of appeal. His great complaint against the Jews was, 'Haven't you read?' Ignorance of Scripture was what had caused the Sadducees to go astray, while the Pharisees' problem was that they disregarded Scripture. And then to some of his own disciples after the resurrection he had to say, 'How foolish you are, and how slow to believe all that the prophets have spoken! Did not the Messiah have to suffer these things and then enter his glory?' Then, continues Luke, 'Beginning with Moses and all the Prophets, he explained to them what was said in all the Scriptures concerning himself.'[13]

This personal submission to Scripture and this recommendation of Scripture to others came down to his belief that what Scripture said, God said. While he referred to the human authors, he took it for granted that there was a single divine Author behind them all. He could equally say 'Moses said' or 'God said'. He could quote a comment of the narrator in Genesis 2:24 as an utterance of the Creator himself. Similarly he said, 'Isaiah was right when he prophesied about you',[14] when what he then went on to quote is the direct speech of the Lord God. It is from Jesus himself that the New Testament authors gained their belief in the dual authorship of Scripture. For them it was just as true to say that 'God spoke to our ancestors through the prophets'[15] as it was to say that 'prophets, though human, spoke from God as they were carried along by the Holy Spirit'.[16] God did not speak in such a way as to obliterate the personality of the human authors, nor did those who wrote the Bible corrupt the Word of the divine Author. God spoke. Human authors spoke. Neither truth must be allowed to detract from the other.

So Jesus Christ endorsed the authority of the Old Testament. There is no occasion on which he contradicted it, or gave the slightest hint that he questioned its divine origin. His only condemnation was of people's ignorance and distortion of it. He also made provision for the writing of the New Testament, by appointing the Twelve (to whom after the resurrection he added Paul) to be his 'apostles' or special delegates, giving them three years' intensive training and eyewitness experience, investing them with his personal authority, sending them out to teach in his name and promising them an extraordinary inspiration of the Spirit to help them recall what he had taught them and to lead them into all the truth.

So the Christian accepts the Bible because of Christ. Christ himself thought of Scripture in terms of a divine word or testimony.

Returning to John 5:39, 40, the quarrel which Jesus had with the Jews was not over their *view* of Scripture, but over their *use* of it. They too accepted its divine *origin* (although God's Word did not 'dwell' in them, v. 38). But they misunderstood its purpose. We need now to consider what the Jews were doing and then what they ought to have been doing. In this way we shall see the contrast between the wrong and the right use of Scripture.

The wrong use of Scripture
First, what the Jews were actually doing is an example of the wrong use of Scripture.

'You study the Scriptures diligently,' Jesus said (v. 39). What could be wrong with that? We shall see.

The Jews of that day were meticulous students of Scripture. They knew that they were greatly privileged to have been 'entrusted with the very words of God'.[17] God had not done this for any other nation; 'they do not know his laws.'[18] So Israel prized the Scriptures highly, rejoicing at God's Word 'like one who finds great spoil',[19] finding it 'more precious than gold, than much pure gold' and 'sweeter than honey, than honey from the honeycomb'.[20]

This led them to study the Scriptures diligently. The Greek word is used in the New Testament of God and Christ searching people's hearts and of the Holy Spirit searching the depths of God. It expresses the most careful perseverance. Surely, we may ask, wasn't this all entirely admirable? Isn't it right and necessary to study the Scriptures? Wouldn't it be good if we ourselves were as enthusiastic in our study of Scripture as they were? Yes indeed. But it is not for this that Jesus criticized them.

Their mistake comes to light when we read the rest of Christ's sentence: 'You study the Scriptures diligently because you think that in them you have eternal life.' The complaint of Jesus is expressed not so much in the words 'you study' as in the words 'you think'. He does not criticize them because they studied the Scriptures, but because they regarded their study as an end in itself. They misunderstood Scripture's God-intended function, which is to point beyond itself to Christ.

The word for 'study' points to what the scholar Bishop Westcott described as 'that minute, intense investigation of Scripture which issued in the allegorical and mystical interpretations of the *Midrash*'. The teachers of the law, for example, whose job was to copy and teach the sacred text, subjected it to the closest scrutiny. They weighed its every syllable. They went so far as to count up the number of words, even letters, of each book. And they did all this, not just for the sake of accurate copying but because they foolishly imagined that eternal life consisted in such accurate knowledge. Like some modern Bible commentators and Bible readers, they became so absorbed in the *words* that they lost sight of the *truth* which the words expressed. They were not concerned about the *message* of Scripture (they did not understand this, let alone embrace and obey it), but only about *meanings*. If they could study and know and memorize and quote the Word of God, they thought that they had eternal life.

These contemporaries of Jesus were not like the noble Jews of Berea we read about later in the New Testament.[21] They were not content merely with examining the Scriptures daily, but did this with the aim of finding out 'if what Paul said was true'.

Clearly they intended, if they were convinced, to put their trust in the Christ whom Paul was proclaiming. But the Jews to whom Jesus spoke had no such excellent reason for studying the Scriptures. They simply studied the Scriptures. They imagined that having Scripture was the same as having life. Their study was an end in itself. In this they were badly mistaken.

The right use of Scripture

Having considered the wrong use of Scripture, we are now ready to turn to the right use of Scripture. The next phrase in what Jesus says makes this clear: 'These are the very Scriptures that testify about me, yet you refuse to come to me to have life.' In these words the purpose of Scripture is made plain. Far from being an end in itself, Scripture is a means to the end of finding life in Christ. It therefore bears witness to Christ, so that people will come to Christ for life. Yet the Jews had missed both these points.

First, they should have seen Christ in Scripture. We have already seen that the biblical testimony is *divine* testimony; we must now see that it is divine testimony *to Christ*. Indeed, the three Persons of the Trinity are all involved in Scripture, for Scripture is the Father's testimony to the Son through the Spirit.

Jesus was, of course, referring to the Old Testament. The Old Testament is a book of hope, of unfulfilled expectation. From beginning to end it looks forward to Christ. Its many promises through Abraham, Moses and the prophets are fulfilled in Christ. Its law, with its unbending demands, was our 'guardian until Christ came',[22] keeping us confined and under restraint, even in bondage, until Christ should set us free. Its sacrificial system, teaching that without the shedding of blood there could be no forgiveness, looked forward to the unique blood-shedding of the Lamb of God. Its kings, for all their imperfections, anticipated the Messiah's perfect reign of righteousness and peace. And its prophecies are all focused on him. Thus Jesus Christ is the seed of the woman who would bruise the serpent's head, the offspring of Abraham through whom all the families of the earth would be blessed, the star that would come out of Jacob and the sceptre that would rise out of Israel. Jesus Christ is also the priest after the order of Melchizedek, the king of David's line, the servant of the Lord God who would suffer and die for the sins of the people, the Son of God who would inherit the nations, and the Son of man, coming with the clouds of heaven, to whom would be given dominion, glory and a kingdom, that all peoples, nations and languages should serve him for ever. Directly or indirectly Jesus Christ is the great theme of the Old Testament. This is how he was able to explain to his disciples 'what was said in all the Scriptures concerning himself'.[23]

It was an amazing privilege for the contemporaries of Jesus to witness the fulfilment of all this accumulated prophecy. 'Blessed are your eyes,' Jesus could say to his disciples, 'because they see, and your ears because they hear. For truly I tell you, many prophets and righteous people longed to see what you see but did not see it, and to hear what you hear but did not hear it.'[24] But the unbelieving Jews did not see him. They did not even see him in Scripture. For all their enthusiastic study of the Scriptures, they missed the Scriptures' chief subject.

If Christ is the heart of the Old Testament, this is even more obvious in the New. The Gospels describe his earthly career, his virgin birth and sinless life, his gracious words and mighty works, his sin-bearing death, his glorious resurrection and ascension. The book of Acts describes his gift of the Spirit on the Day of Pentecost, and what he continued to do and to teach by his Spirit through his apostles. The Epistles unfold more fully

the extraordinary glory of his divine-human Person, saving work
and coming kingdom, and tell us how we should live in the
light of these truths. The Revelation lifts our eyes beyond earth
and history, up to heaven where Christ is seen to share God's
eternal throne and on to the end when he will come again in
majesty, take his power and reign. Yet there are some people
who manage to read the whole Bible, New Testament as well as
Old, without realizing that its chief purpose is to tell us about
Jesus Christ!

The Bible is full of Christ. Some of the old English commentators used to put it like this: Just as in England every road,
lane and path, linking on to others, will ultimately lead you to
London, so in the Bible every book, chapter and verse, linking
on to others, will ultimately lead you to Christ.

The Jews' two mistakes

Thus the first tragedy about those Jewish contemporaries of
Christ is that they studied the Scriptures, the very Scriptures
which bear witness to Christ, but failed to see the Christ to
whom the Scriptures bear such constant testimony.

The second tragedy is this: they should have come to Christ
for life. We have seen that the Bible points to Christ. But what
is the purpose of this biblical testimony to him? It is not just
that we should *look at him*, but that we should *go to him* in order
to receive life from him. The true function of Scripture is to
testify to Christ so plainly and powerfully that first we see him,
and secondly we believe in him for life. In this way life comes
through faith, and faith comes through testimony.

John himself emphasizes this towards the end of his Gospel:
'These [i.e. signs] are written that you may believe that Jesus is
the Messiah, the Son of God, and that by believing you may
have life in his name.'[25] The apostle Paul writes something very

similar to Timothy: 'the Holy Scriptures . . . are able to make you wise for salvation through faith in Christ Jesus.'[26] So Christ and his apostles teach the same sequence of events. 'Salvation' or 'life' is in Christ. Therefore the Scriptures set Christ forth as the Saviour, the Giver of life, in order to stimulate our faith in him.

The Jews should have come to Christ to receive life. But they did not. It is partly that they were blind: 'You think' – and think wrongly – Jesus said, that life is in the Scriptures. But it is especially that they were stubborn: 'you refuse to come to me to have life.' These words of Christ are very revealing, this 'you think' and 'you refuse'. They show that the controlling factor in our behaviour is not only our reason and our understanding, but our will. Perhaps these Jews were using theology to rational- ize their sinful unwillingness to come to Christ.

We can now see the tragic foolishness of their second mistake. They were using the Scriptures as an end instead of as a means to an end. Their view of Scripture was academic instead of practical. They imagined they could find eternal life in the Scriptures. But the truth is that eternal life can only be found in the Christ to whom the Scriptures testify.

A simple illustration may help to show the extreme stupidity of the Jews, and of all readers of the Bible who never look beyond it to Christ. Supposing we decide one day to go on a family picnic to a beauty spot such as Box Hill in Surrey. We get into the car and drive off in the direction of our chosen destination. After a while we come to the signpost marked 'Box Hill'. What now? Do we immediately stop the car, get out and have our picnic round the signpost? Of course not. The idea is ridiculous. We follow the signpost to Box Hill and have our picnic there.

Now the Bible is a signpost – not to Box Hill, but to Calvary's Hill, where Christ died for sinners. It shows us the way to God, to forgiveness, to heaven, to holiness, because it points us to Christ who is the way to all these. True, we often gather round the Scriptures in Christian fellowship. But we do not stop there. We do not have our picnic round the signpost. Christ, not the Bible, is the object of our faith and the centre of our fellowship.

So evangelical Christians are not bibliolaters. If we value the Scriptures very highly (which we do), this is not for themselves, but because they are the Father's testimony to Christ. A young man will treasure his girlfriend's photographs and letters, but only because they speak to him of the one he loves. So too Christians love the Bible, because it is Christ's portrait and speaks to us of him.

To suppose that salvation lies in a book is as foolish as supposing that health lies in a prescription. When we are ill and our doctor prescribes some medicine, is the intention that we should go home with the prescription, read it, study it and learn it by heart? Or that we should frame it and hang it on our bedroom wall? Or that we tear it into fragments and eat the pieces three times a day after meals? The absurdity of these possibilities is obvious. The prescription itself will not cure us. No, the whole purpose of a prescription is to get us to go to the chemist, obtain the medicine prescribed for us and take it. Now the Bible contains the divine prescription for sin-sick souls. It specifies the only medicine which can save us from perishing. In brief, it tells us of Jesus Christ who died for us and rose again. But we do not worship the Bible as if it could save us; we go to Christ. For the overriding purpose of the Bible is to send us to Christ and persuade us to take the water of life which he offers.

What Christ said about the Scriptures is equally true of the sacraments, namely Baptism and the Lord's Supper. Their function and purpose are the same. Both the Scriptures and the sacraments are God-given signposts (the Scriptures in written words, the sacraments in visible words or pictures) which direct our attention away from themselves to Christ. Verbally in Scripture, visually in sacrament, Jesus Christ is proclaimed as the only Saviour of sinners. But neither Scripture nor sacrament is an end in itself. Both are means to an end, namely that we find salvation in Christ. Both are means of grace, ways in which God's grace is offered to us, because they reveal Christ to us and strengthen our faith in him. Indeed, 'the sacraments function as a means of *grace* because, and only because, God uses them, as he uses his Word, as a means to *faith*.'[27] So the evangelical should consistently reject any suggestion that reading the Bible or receiving the sacraments of Baptism or Holy Communion brings any automatic blessing. The reading and preaching of God's Word doesn't do any good to a congregation unless those who hear respond in faith. And the sacraments are of no benefit to those who don't believe. Since they are 'visible words', they also must be met with faith.

To become engrossed in a book on the one hand, or in bread, wine and water on the other, is to overturn the God-ordained function of both Scripture and sacrament. It is just as possible to have superstitious views of the Bible as it is to have superstitious views of the consecrated elements at Communion. But we should not fall into this trap. This is not to say that we do not value both Scriptures and sacraments very highly. We do. We do not forget that both come from God. But we also remember that God has given us them in order to display Christ before the eyes of our heart, to attract our attention to him and to draw out our faith in him.

When somebody first handles a pair of binoculars, never having seen such a thing before, they may well misuse them by looking *at* them, not realizing that their purpose is to look *through* them in order to see more clearly what they are looking at. In the same way people can misunderstand the purpose of Scripture and sacrament. They are binoculars for the magnification of Jesus Christ. We are to look through them, not at them. Our focus is to be on Christ.

The need for obedience

How, then, shall we avoid making the same foolish mistakes as the Jews back in our Lord's day? It will be helpful to remind ourselves of certain simple facts.

First, it is not enough to *possess* a Bible. It is extraordinary how much primitive superstition lurks in the human heart. There are people whose only acquaintance with the Bible is that they have a copy on a bookshelf somewhere. They suppose that its presence there somehow adds something special to the home. Maybe it has sentimental value because it is a family heirloom or Sunday school prize or Confirmation present. Some speak of it with reverence as the 'Holy Bible'.

Next, it is not enough to *read* the Bible, or hear it read in church. Neither public nor private Bible reading is to be an end in itself. There is no value in the reading of Scripture for its own sake, but only if it effectively introduces us to Jesus Christ. There is nothing special in reading it as great literature either. The Bible was never 'designed to be read as literature'; it was designed by God as a testimony to Christ to persuade us to go to him. Whenever the Bible is read, in private, in family prayers or in church, what is needed is an eager expectation that through it we may meet Christ.

Thirdly, it is not enough to *study* the Bible. Some Christians 'study the Scriptures' today, like the Jews of old. They find it a fascinating textbook. They pride themselves on how much they know. Like Apollos in Acts 18, they have 'a thorough knowledge of the Scriptures'.[28] They have read it many times from cover to cover and committed large sections of it to memory. Fine! But to accumulate Bible knowledge is one thing; a growing personal knowledge of Jesus Christ, whom to know is eternal life, is quite another.

No. What is required is that we *obey* the Bible. The best way to honour this book as God's book is to do what it says. And if we do what it says, we shall keep coming to Christ for the supply of all our needs. We shall never be satisfied with merely studying the Scriptures; we shall search for Christ in the Scriptures and go on searching until we find him. Then he will never need to rebuke us in the way in which he rebuked his Jewish contemporaries by saying, 'You study the Scriptures. You read a set passage every day. You even memorize verses and call yourself a Bible student. But you will not come to *me* for life.'

From the verses which we have been considering in John 5, Jesus indicates that the Scriptures have both a divine origin and a practical purpose. We learn their divine origin from Christ's testimony to them. We learn their practical purpose from their testimony to Christ. There is therefore between Christ (the living Word) and Scripture (the written Word) this two-way testimony. Each bears witness to the other. Because Christ bears witness to Scripture, we believe it. Because Scripture bears witness to Christ, we go to him.

4

Salvation: Merit or mercy?

Two of the most basic issues of religion concern authority and salvation, the source of authority and the means of salvation. These are the two questions every religious person is bound to ask. First, how can I know what to believe? Secondly, how can I be put right with God? These questions are to some extent common to all religions. The very fact that they are asked at all assumes a degree of common understanding about human limitations – of mind (since we are finite, how can we know God?) and of character (since we are sinful, how can we reach God?).

The divine initiative

The Christian answer to both questions is to direct the en-quirer's attention to God himself, and to affirm that God has taken the initiative to do for us what we could not do for ourselves. By what authority can I know what is true? Answer: because God has *said* something. By what means can I be saved? Answer: because God has *done* something. The Christian word for this divine initiative is 'grace'. Grace is God's love to those who do not deserve it. Grace is love that cares and stoops and rescues. Before going any further, let us consider certain aspects of this double divine initiative of grace.

First, the divine initiative belongs in one sense to the past. It began back in eternity, progressively unfolded in the history of Israel, the nation God chose to be his people, and culminated in the coming of Jesus Christ. In him God's initiative reached its climax – in one sense one could say its conclusion.

This truth regarding the finality of God's initiative in Christ is conveyed by one word in the Greek Testament, namely *hapax* and its variant *ephapax*. It is usually translated as 'once for all'. It is applied in the New Testament to both revelation and redemption. Thus, Jude refers to 'the faith that was *once for all* entrusted to God's holy people'.[1] The apostles Paul and Peter, on the other hand, and the unknown author of the Epistle to the Hebrews, use the word *hapax* to describe the atoning death of Christ. For example, 'The death he died, he died to sin *once for all*.'[2] 'For Christ also suffered *once* for sins.'[3] Again, 'he has appeared *once for all* at the culmination of the ages to do away with sin by the sacrifice of himself. Just as people are destined to die once, and after that to face judgment, so Christ was sacrificed *once* to take away the sins of many; and he will appear a second time . . . '[4]

We can put it like this: God has spoken once for all and Christ has suffered once for all. This means that the Christian revelation and the Christian redemption are both complete in Christ. Nothing can be added to either without belittling Christ, either the unique glory of his divine–human Person or the absolute adequacy of his saving work. These are the two rocks on which the Protestant Reformation was built – God's revealed Word without the addition of human traditions and Christ's finished work without the addition of human merit. The Reformers' great watchwords were *sola scriptura* for our authority and *sola gratia* for our salvation.

Secondly, the divine initiative belongs also in the present. Although what God said and did in Christ was *finished* in the past, it is not *buried* in the past. Although it is final, it is also contemporary. For the fruits of God's finished word and work in Christ may be gathered and enjoyed today. Indeed, it is the special work of the Holy Spirit in these days of the New Covenant to do exactly that, namely to apply to believers in the present the riches of Christ's word and work in the past. It is through the Spirit that God makes happen now what he finished in Christ. The Holy Spirit enlightens our minds to grasp what God has *said* in Christ and stirs up our faith to grasp what God has *done* in Christ.

We need to emphasize that what the Spirit speaks he speaks through what has already been spoken, and that what the Spirit does he does through what has already been done. There is no new revelation, but an unfolding understanding of what God revealed in Christ (and in the apostolic witness to Christ). There is no fresh redemption, but a progressive taking up of what God achieved in Christ.

Thirdly, the divine initiative in both these areas (revelation and redemption) and in both their aspects (finished and contemporary) is supernatural. This is why we began in chapter 1 by asking whether the Christian religion is natural or supernatural. It was an essential introduction to questions about authority and salvation that followed. What God said and did in the historical Christ involved events which were unashamedly and inescapably supernatural. The incarnation, including the virgin birth as the way God chose to make it happen, the mighty works, the atonement, the resurrection, the ascension and the

coming of the Spirit – these cannot be explained in natural or
human terms. And the same is true of what God says and does
through the Spirit today. If we understand the truth as it is in
Jesus, this is not because of our own cleverness, but because of
divine illumination: 'this was not revealed to you by flesh and
blood, but by my Father in heaven';[5] ' . . . God, who set me
apart from my mother's womb . . . was pleased to reveal his Son
in me';[6] 'For God, who said, "Let light shine out of darkness,"
made his light shine in our hearts to give us the light of the
knowledge of God's glory displayed in the face of Christ';[7] 'no
one can say, "Jesus is Lord," except by the Holy Spirit'.[8]

In the same way, if we have become new people in Christ,
redeemed and recreated, it is not because of any human resolve
or effort of our own, but because of divine grace: 'For it is by
grace you have been saved, through faith – and this is not from
yourselves, it is the gift of God – not by works, so that no one
can boast. For we are God's handiwork, created in Christ Jesus
to do good works . . . ';[9] 'All this is from God, who reconciled
us to himself through Christ . . . '[10]

Having thought about some of the parallels between authority
and salvation, and the way the same divine initiative of grace is
at work in both, we are now able to turn our attention to
salvation.

Salvation and justification

Christianity is a religion of salvation. It is a word that is rather
unfashionable today and there are some in the church too
squeamish to use it. But the fact that it causes either amuse-
ment or embarrassment to many only demonstrates how
far the modern church has drifted from the religion of the
Bible, the whole of which is the story of salvation. Salvation in
Christ, the way in which the living God has taken action in his

grace to search out and to save humanity, is the one theme which runs through Scripture from beginning to end.

What, then, is 'salvation'? It is a great word which urgently needs to be set free from the narrow ideas to which it has often been reduced. Salvation is not just another word for forgiveness. It is much bigger and broader than that. It represents God's total plan for humanity, and it includes at least three phases. Phase one is our deliverance from the guilt and judgment of our sins, our free and full forgiveness, together with our reconciliation to God and our adoption as his children. Phase two is our progressive liberation from the ability of evil to drag us down, beginning with our new birth into the family of God and continuing with our transformation by the Spirit of Christ into the image of Christ. Phase three is our final deliverance from the sin which lingers both in our fallen nature and in our social environment, when on the last day we shall be given new and glorious bodies and transferred to a new heaven and a new earth.

These three phases, or tenses, of salvation (past, present and future) are associated in the New Testament with the three major events in the saving career of Jesus, his death, his resurrection and the subsequent gift of the Spirit, and his return in power and glory. Paul calls them justification, sanctification and glorification.

For the moment we will concentrate on the first phase, 'justification', and reflect on how Christ dealt with the subject in another of his controversies with the Pharisees. We saw in chapter 2 how he accused them of 'nullifying the word of God through their tradition'. In this chapter we shall see how they were just as skilled at cancelling out God's work of redemption. Christ's quarrel with them now is not that they had an inflated respect for their own traditions, but that they had an exaggerated confidence in their own merits. His criticism of them is expressed clearly in his parable of the Pharisee and the tax collector.

> To some who were confident of their own righteousness and looked down on everyone else, Jesus told this parable: 'Two men went up to the temple to pray, one a Pharisee and the other a tax collector. The Pharisee stood by himself and prayed: "God, I thank you that I am not like other people – robbers, evildoers, adulterers – or even like this tax collector. I fast twice a week and give a tenth of all I get." But the tax collector stood at a distance. He would not even look up to heaven, but beat his breast and said, "God, have mercy on me, a sinner." I tell you that this man, rather than the other, went home justified before God. For all those who exalt themselves will be humbled, and those who humble themselves will be exalted.'[11]

Perhaps the best approach to an understanding of this parable is to begin at the end with the word 'justified' (v. 14). It is with this single word that Jesus summed up the great blessing which the tax collector received and the Pharisee missed out on. It's true that we normally associate the vocabulary of justification with the apostle Paul. But Paul's teaching is already anticipated here, and it is quite wrong to attempt to drive a wedge between Jesus and Paul in this (or any other) doctrine. There are two further occurrences in Luke's Gospel of the verb 'to justify', both relating to self-justification: the first of the lawyer who 'wanted to justify himself'[12] and the second of the Pharisees whom Jesus similarly described as those who 'justify yourselves in the eyes of others'.[13]

That Jesus should have used the word 'justification' is not at all surprising, because it occurs quite frequently in the Old Testament. 'Justification' is a legal word, a technical term borrowed from the law courts. It is best understood from its opposite, 'condemnation'. The Old Testament magistrates were instructed to justify the righteous and to condemn the wicked; that is, to pronounce the innocent person innocent and the guilty person guilty. And they were told that 'Acquitting the guilty and condemning the innocent – the Lord detests them both'.[14]

This Old Testament background is sufficient to indicate the shock and anger the Pharisees must have felt when they heard Jesus say that the sinful tax collector 'went home justified before God'. How could Jesus tolerate such a miscarriage of justice? Was he not daring to claim that God had done something which Scripture said was detestable to him? Had God not categorically stated in Exodus, 'I will not acquit the guilty'?[15] How then could anybody possibly say that he 'justifies the ungodly'? – which, incidentally, is exactly what Paul says in Romans that he regularly does.[16]

These are fundamental questions about salvation. The answer to them is supplied in embryo in the parable and fully developed in the rest of the New Testament. To understand it, we need first to look at the two men who figure in it. They represent two groups with whom Jesus was in constant touch throughout his public ministry.

The Pharisee and the tax collector contrasted

Tax collectors were widely despised on both political and moral grounds. They were employed by the hated Romans and so were regarded as political collaborators. And they tended to rely for their livelihood on whatever extra they could extort from their helpless victims beyond the tax they were entitled to charge.

The Pharisees, on the other hand, were almost as universally popular as the tax collectors were despised. Their views on religion and ethics were accepted by the great majority of their fellow citizens. Both politically and morally they were as strict as the tax collectors were lax. They refused to compromise with the Roman occupation, and they were determined to keep themselves free from all defilement as they understood it. They 'preached the keeping of the Law, and the coming world of blessedness as the reward of obedience . . . All this made the Pharisees more and more proud, formal and uncharitable. They despised the common people.'[17] An example of how confident they were in their own righteousness for salvation is found in the so-called *Psalms of Solomon*: 'To do right and wrong is in the work of our hands.'[18]

In the parable which Jesus told, the two actors have much in common. Both 'went up to the temple to pray'. Both stood to pray, as the Jews normally did. Both prayed. Both began their prayer with the same word, 'God'.

But there the similarities between them ended. When we look below the surface, they were separated from each other by four major differences.

First, they had an entirely different *opinion of themselves*. This was expressed in how they prayed. The Pharisee said, 'God, I . . . I . . . I . . . I . . . I'. He used the personal pronoun five times in his brief speech. The tax collector also used the personal pronoun – once – but not in the same way. He did not regard himself as a subject who had done or could do anything to win God's kindness, or who even had a right to address God at all. He saw himself rather as the needy *object* of the divine mercy: 'God, have mercy on *me*, a sinner!'

The opinion which each man had of himself is further illustrated by the fact that each placed himself in a category by himself. The Pharisee begins: 'God, I thank you that I am not like other people.' Luke has prepared us for his arrogance with his introduction: 'He also told this parable to some who trusted in themselves that they were righteous and despised others.' We know from the Talmud that this was not an exaggerated sentiment for Jesus to have put into the mouth of a Pharisee. There we can read of a certain Rabbi Simeon ben Jochai who used to say, 'I have seen the children of the world to come, and they are few. If there are three, I and my son are of their number; if they are two, I and my son are they.'[19]

The tax collector also saw himself as unique – not in virtue, however, but in sin. 'God, have mercy on me, a sinner,' he said, literally '*the* sinner'. He was so vividly aware of his own short-comings that he made no odious comparisons between himself and others. He was conscious only of his personal need for mercy. This is the language of true remorse. The apostle Paul, the converted Pharisee, was the same. He called himself 'the worst of sinners',[20] whom Christ Jesus had come to save.

The Pharisee sought to draw God's attention to what he saw as his outstanding merit. The tax collector, on the other hand, avoided going into details; to call himself 'the sinner' was enough.

Secondly, their different opinion of themselves was reflected in their different *posture in prayer*. Both men 'stood' in customary Jewish fashion. But their attitude was not the same. The Pharisee stood up straight, proud and ostentatious, and though he called upon God in words, he was actually praying 'by himself'. The tax collector, however, was seen 'standing at a distance'. Presumably he had not thought it appropriate to enter the Temple itself. He did not consider himself fit to stand in God's house. He probably stayed outside, in one of the Temple courts. There he 'would not even look up to heaven, but beat his breast and said, "God, have mercy on me, a sinner."' Using just a few words, Jesus seems to indicate that every part of the tax collector's body expressed his humble penitence. His feet kept their distance from the holy place; like Moses at the burning bush he knew himself unfit to come near. His eyes looked down to the ground in shame; he could have echoed Ezra's prayer, 'I am too ashamed and disgraced, my God, to lift up my face to you.'[21] His hands struck his breast mournfully, acknowledging his guilt, as the Jews still do in the most solemn part of their confession on the Day of Atonement. And from his mouth came words of deep contrition and penitence.

Given their different opinion of themselves expressed in their different posture, it is no surprise to read, thirdly, of their different *standing before God*. 'I tell you,' Jesus concluded with deliberate emphasis, 'that this man, rather than the other, went home justified before God.' The Pharisee was condemned, while the tax collector was justified. In their present standing and their final destiny they were as different as heaven and hell.

And this was because of the fourth and fundamental difference between these men, namely the different *source of their confidence*.

In order to understand this fully, we need to realize that the assessment each man gave of himself (at least externally in the Pharisee's case) was accurate. They were not lying or even exaggerating. The Pharisee was what he said he was, both religious and righteous. As far as his religion was concerned, he had indeed gone to the Temple to pray, he fasted, and he tithed his money. And these three – prayer, fasting and giving – were accepted as the three chief religious duties. Jesus himself in the Sermon on the Mount made it clear that he expected his own disciples to pray, to fast and to give. The Pharisee even went beyond the requirements of the law. The law said that Jews had to fast *twice a year* (on the Day of Atonement and the day commemorating the destruction of Solomon's Temple); the Pharisee fasted '*twice a week*'. The law said that Jews had to give away a tenth of their produce, i.e. from what they had grown and from their livestock; the Pharisee could claim, 'I give a tenth of all that I get.' By doing so he was faithfully observing one of his vows, for it was said of the Pharisee in the Mishnah that he 'tithes all that he eats, all that he sells, and all that he buys'.

As for the Pharisee's righteousness, there is no need to doubt that he was telling the truth when he declared himself neither a robber, nor an evildoer, nor an adulterer. He had not broken the commandments of God about honesty and immorality – at least not externally in what he had done.

So, in both religion and morals, this Pharisee in Christ's story will have appeared to his contemporaries (as indeed he appeared to himself) to be a wholly admirable person.

The tax collector, on the other hand, was despicable. He called himself 'a sinner', '*the* sinner'. And there is no reason to doubt that he too was exactly what he said he was. He was politically and morally disreputable.

So how in the name of justice can Jesus have declared the righteous Pharisee condemned and the unrighteous tax collector justified?

We begin to get an answer to our question when we notice this: the Pharisee was not condemned because he was righteous, but because he was self-righteous. His righteousness in any case was external only. 'God knows the heart.' If the Pharisee could have seen his own heart, he would have known immediately that his confidence in himself had no basis.

Similarly, the tax collector was not justified because he was a sinner but because, having admitted that he was a sinner, guilty and deserving of judgment, he called on God for mercy.

In a word, both men were sinners, deserving judgment. But only one admitted it and called on God to have mercy on him.

This is why Jesus had to say to the Pharisees, 'Truly I tell you, the tax collectors and the prostitutes are entering the kingdom of God ahead of you.'[22] Not because they were tax collectors and prostitutes (sin in itself gives no one the right to enter God's kingdom), but because they humbled themselves by recognizing their sin, and then repenting and believing.

So this fourth difference between the Pharisee and the tax collector was the really basic one. It concerned the object of their confidence for salvation. The Pharisee was confident of his own righteousness and looked down on everyone else (v. 9). The tax collector was so conscious of his own guilt that he forgot others and relied completely on the mercy of God.

Indeed, the more one thinks about these two men, the clearer it becomes that they had entirely opposite ideas of how a person can be confident about how they stand with God. The Pharisee's view of his own righteousness was so exaggerated that he thought he was a proper subject not for prayer, still less for penitence, but actually for thanksgiving! 'God, I thank you,' he began. Taken out of their context and considered in themselves, these words make a promising beginning to any prayer. If only he had continued, 'I thank you that you are such a great God', or 'that you have so richly provided me with everything for my enjoyment', all would have been well. Instead, he thanked God for his own merits. A similar self-righteousness was found in Rabbi Simon who even claimed that, if Abraham's righteousness had redeemed all generations up to his time, he would redeem by his own merits all that followed him until the end of the world!

What of the tax collector's confidence? He was undoubtedly ashamed of his past and sincerely wanted to be a better person. But it didn't occur to him to use his penitence or future resolve as reasons for God to accept him. No. He had sinned against

God. Only divine mercy could save him from the divine judgment he knew he deserved. And in this mercy of God he put his trust, knowing from the Old Testament that the Lord is 'the compassionate and gracious God, slow to anger, abounding in love and faithfulness'.[23]

The difference between them was this: the Pharisee appealed for justice on the ground of his supposed merit, while the tax collector acknowledged his entire lack of merit and appealed for mercy alone. Jesus summed up this contrast with one of his favourite sayings: 'all those who exalt themselves will be humbled, and those who humble themselves will be exalted' (v. 11).

Mercy not merit

It is significant that the parable is immediately followed (in vv. 15–17) by the incident in which children were brought to Jesus. When the disciples saw it, they showed that they had been infected with the attitude of the Pharisees by rebuking the adults who brought them. They had not yet learned that the humble dependence of a little child was the essential condition of acceptance with God and precisely what the Pharisees lacked. So Jesus called the disciples to him and said, 'Let the little children come to me, and do not hinder them, for the kingdom of God belongs to such as these.'

This is how Jesus taught, emphasizing the givenness, the freeness of salvation. The so-called 'unmerciful servant' in the parable[24] was so heavily in debt to his master that 'he was not able to pay'; his master then out of pity 'cancelled the debt and let him go'. The forgiveness of God is a gift to be received, not a reward to be merited. 'If you knew the gift of God,' he had said earlier to the Samaritan woman, 'and who it is that asks you for a drink, you would have asked him and he would have given you living water.'[25] And again, this time to the Jews who did not believe in him: 'Do not work for food that spoils, but for food that endures to eternal life, which the Son of Man will give you.'[26] 'What must we do to do the works God requires?' they went on to ask. Jesus replied, 'The work of God is this: to believe in the one he has sent.' It is the same as the contrast he draws in the parable of the Pharisee and the tax collector. Eternal life is a gift, not a wage. It is free, not earned. It doesn't become ours by 'doing' or 'working', but by 'receiving' or 'believing'. The way of salvation is by faith, not works.

The same basic distinction between the two objects of confidence or boasting (human merit and divine mercy) is most strikingly illustrated in the New Testament by the career of Saul of Tarsus, the Pharisee who became a Christian. 'We . . . boast in Christ Jesus,' he writes, 'and put no confidence in the flesh',[27] thus setting the two stages of his career in stark contrast, first as Saul the Pharisee who put his confidence in the flesh, and now as Paul the Christian who boasts in Christ Jesus alone. By 'the flesh' he meant everything he was in himself and by himself – what his parents and teachers had made him and what he considered he had succeeded in making himself. To put the matter beyond dispute, he goes on to separate out for us the various elements which together made up his 'flesh' – his Jewish ancestry, his Hebrew education, his religion, sincerity, zeal and righteousness.[28] These were precisely the things of which every Pharisee was proud. But then: 'Whatever were gains to me I now consider loss for the sake of *Christ*. What is more, I consider everything a loss because of the surpassing worth of knowing *Christ Jesus* my Lord, for *whose* sake I have lost all things. I consider them garbage, that I may gain *Christ* and be found in *him*, not having a righteousness of my own that comes from the law, but that which is through faith in *Christ* – the righteousness that comes from God on the basis of faith . . . '[29] The sixfold reference to Christ stands out clearly. He had been trusting in himself that he was righteous; he came to put his trust in Christ. Or, as we might equally well put it, he came to rely on the mercy of God displayed in Christ, since there is no significant difference between the tax collector's faith in God's mercy and Saul's faith in Christ.

The significance of Christ's death

Nor is there any distinction in this matter of saving faith between the tax collector and us – except that we know far more about God's mercy than he ever knew. For we live after the death of Christ in which the mercy of God was supremely demonstrated. Today the object of the penitent sinner's confidence for acceptance with God is not divine mercy in general but, very specifically, Jesus Christ and him crucified. For although God's mercy is seen in the whole saving career of Jesus, and although his birth, life, death, resurrection, ascension and gift of the Spirit belong inseparably together in that saving career, yet the New Testament states that what he did to put away our sins was to die. It was on the cross that he bore them in his own body, paying their penalty. It is his 'blood', the symbol of the laying down of his life, which can cleanse us from them today. And only because he died our death is it possible for us to have life. Only because he was made a curse for us can we inherit a blessing. Only because he endured our condemnation may we be justified – if we echo the tax collector's prayer.

Although it is not until the New Testament Epistles that the full implications of the death of Jesus are drawn out, yet the nature and the need of it were already clear in his own mind. He made at least two clear statements about the aim and object of his death. First, he said he had come 'to give his life as a ransom for many'.[30] Secondly, he referred to the Communion cup as his 'blood of the (new) covenant', which would be 'poured out for many for the forgiveness of sins'.[31] Thus it was by the shedding of his blood in a violent, sacrificial death that the promised new covenant or agreement between God and humanity would be established, an agreement whose terms would include both the forgiveness of sin and deliverance from sin. Since this was to be the supreme achievement of his death, it is no wonder that it played such a large part in his thinking. He must suffer, he kept repeating, as Scripture said he would. This was the 'hour' for which he had come into the world. At the same time, he would face this death voluntarily, and nothing would deflect him from his purpose. As the Good Shepherd, he would lay down his life for his sheep. No-one would take his life from him. He would lay it down freely. He had authority to lay it down, and he had authority to take it up again.[32] More than that, through his death he would draw all people, including the Gentiles, to himself. Just as a kernel of wheat must fall into the earth and die before it can produce many seeds, so he would die in order to multiply.[33]

Jesus was so positive about the centrality of his death in the purpose of God that he instituted his special Supper for its continual commemoration. It is highly significant that the only regular ritual act instituted and commanded by Jesus focuses chiefly on his death. It is his *death*, his body given and his blood shed, which the bread and wine were intended to signify. In issuing the command to 'do this in remembrance' of him, he intended that his atoning death should be kept before every generation, displayed clearly before everyone. According to Paul, this is the function of preaching.[34] It is also one of the functions of Communion. The ministry of both word and sacrament brings Christ's death into the present, offering it anew not to

God (for the sacrifice itself was offered on the cross once for all) but to us (for its benefits are always freshly available).

During his ministry, when Christ presented himself to people as the object of their faith, he did so as their sacrificed Saviour. Let us consider two striking examples. First, 'as Moses lifted up the snake in the wilderness, so the Son of Man must be lifted up, that everyone who believes may have eternal life in him'.[35] Secondly, 'Very truly I tell you, unless you eat the flesh of the Son of Man and drink his blood, you have no life in you. Whoever eats my flesh and drinks my blood has eternal life . . . '[36] Saving faith, therefore, is gazing at the Son of man lifted up on the cross; it is eating the flesh and drinking the blood of the divine victim who has offered himself as a sacrifice for sin.

These vivid metaphors of Jesus do more than illustrate the object of saving faith (Christ crucified); they also demonstrate that there is no merit in faith itself. The power to save lies in the one who is gazed upon, not the one who does the looking. And the ability to nourish rests with the one who is fed upon, not the one who does the eating.

The sacraments of the gospel

If there is no power to save either in our good works or in our faith, there is no power to save in the mere reception of the sacraments either. The sacraments act as a drama of salvation; they do not and cannot by themselves convey it. However, as drama they put across what salvation is and also how it is received.

Take what salvation is. Baptism is a rite of purification. The water of baptism stands for that 'heavenly washing' and that gift of the Spirit which together make up salvation and which Christ died to purchase for us. Similarly, the bread and wine of

Communion are visible, touchable emblems of Christ's body given and blood shed on the cross for our sins. The message that both sacraments preach is the gospel of salvation through Christ crucified.

The sacraments point to how salvation is received as well as what it is. What do candidates for baptism do? Nothing, precisely nothing! Instead, something is done to them. If the baptism is by immersion, they are plunged beneath the water; otherwise, water is poured or sprinkled upon them. In either case they are passive recipients. Nowhere in the New Testament do people ever baptize themselves. Instead, they submit to baptism. From the first baptisms on the Day of Pentecost right up to the present day the same summons has been: 'Repent and be baptized, every one of you, in the name of Jesus Christ for the forgiveness of your sins. And you will receive the gift of the Holy Spirit.'[37] Jesus Christ is the sole giver of forgiveness and of the Holy Spirit. So penitent sinners are baptized in his name, to signify their believing acceptance of Christ's gifts.

It is the same in the Lord's Supper. The drama in the Upper Room did not have just the one actor with eleven in the audience. The apostles were not mere spectators but partici-pants. What was their role? Simply to receive what Christ gave them. He broke the bread; they ate it. He took the cup; they drank it. He thus gave the church both a permanent symbol of his dying sacrifice in the bread and wine, and in the eating and the drinking a permanent picture of saving faith. The Lord's Supper is a visible portrayal of that great saying of Jesus already quoted: 'Whoever eats my flesh and drinks my blood has eternal life, and I will raise them up at the last day.'[38]

Let me repeat that the sacraments dramatize salvation and do not in themselves automatically convey it. Augustine called them *verba visibilia*, 'visible words'. The point is that it is not by the mere outward administration of water in baptism that we are cleansed and receive the Spirit, nor by the mere gift of bread and wine in Communion that we feed on Christ crucified. No, what we need is faith in the promises of God of which these things are a visible expression. What we need is faith demonstrated by our humble, believing acceptance of these signs. But we must not confuse the signs with the promises to which they point. It is possible to receive the sign without receiving the promise, and also to receive the promise apart from the receiving of the sign.

We also deny that we can be invited to worship God in our natural and unredeemed state. The truth is that we have nothing whatever to offer until we have first received. This is why the movement of both gospel sacraments, like the movement of the gospel itself, is primarily towards humanity in grace. In the Lord's Supper we do not and cannot in any sense offer Christ or participate in his self-offering; instead we receive him, spiritually and by faith. It is only *after* we have received, and as a result of having received, that we offer ourselves, our souls and bodies, as a living sacrifice to God.

Apart from this responsive offering of ourselves, sacrificial language is quite inappropriate in connection with the Communion Service, and the Anglican Reformers carefully eliminated it from the Prayer Book. They replaced 'altar' by 'the Lord's Table' or 'Communion Table', and retained 'priest' only because the English word is a contraction of 'presbyter' and translates the Greek word *presbyteros* (elder), not *hiereus* (sacrificing priest). The person who officiates at Holy Communion is not a priest who makes a sacrifice on an altar; he is a minister who serves supper from a table. And those who come to receive come primarily as beggars, like the tax collector. We declare ourselves unworthy even to gather up the crumbs under Christ's table. The giving of ourselves to his service follows on from, and is entirely dependent upon, our receiving God's generosity.

Justification and its fruits

The biblical way of salvation is clear. As with the Pharisee and the tax collector, as with Saul who became Paul, so too with us: God accepts us sinners not because of anything we do or any quality we possess, but because of his own mercy, on the basis of Christ's completed work, in which by grace we put our trust.

This trust in the finished work of Christ, which is the route to justification, leads to two further blessings on which evangelical Christians have always joyfully insisted. The first is 'the priesthood of all believers'.

In Old Testament days the priests were a distinct caste, enjoying privileges which were denied to the people in general. In particular, they offered the sacrifices which the ordinary people were not allowed to offer. They enjoyed access to God in Tabernacle or Temple, while the people stayed outside. This priest–people distinction is done away in Christ. He offered one sacrifice for sins for ever and then entered the presence of God. Now he makes all his people 'priests'.[39] As such, 'we have confidence to enter the Most Holy Place' – all of us, from the greatest to the least without distinction – 'by the blood of Jesus'.[40] There is no further sacrifice for sin to offer – since Christ's single sin-offering was sufficient to put away all sin. Yet there are sacrifices of praise, thanksgiving and dedication which as 'a holy priesthood' we should be offering to God continuously.[41]

If the priesthood of all believers is the first fruit of justification, 'assurance' is the second, that is to say, the God-given certainty that through Christ our sins really have been forgiven, we have peace with God and he has given us eternal life. Such assurance is not arrogant presumption, since it does not depend on us but simply on the completed work of Christ who bore our sins and bought our salvation.

Some objections

Despite its great and wonderful blessings, the way of salvation which Jesus Christ and his apostles proclaimed, as a gift of mercy not an award for merit, has had many outspoken critics. And so as we end this chapter, let us weigh some of the chief objections to it.

1. It is said to be *dishonest.* The dishonesty is said to belong not to God's part in the transaction, but to ours. 'How can we take our place beside that tax collector and echo what he says about being a miserable sinner?' 'This is surely the exaggerated language of the religious past,' the objector continues. 'It no longer rings true today.'

No? Well, all I can say is that it should! If I cannot make the tax collector's prayer my own, it simply shows that I am still a Pharisee. But once the Holy Spirit has done his work of convincing us sinners of our sins, we will have no difficulty with what the tax collector says. Humility before God is nothing but the truth. It is an accurate assessment of myself rather than an artificial pretence. When we begin to see ourselves as God sees us – in defiance of his authority, in rebellion against his love, self-centred and proud – then we shall recognize that the language of the tax collector, far from being dishonest, is the only possible language to use.

2. It is said to be *morbid.* 'Your doctrine of justification puts a most unfortunate emphasis on sin,' we are told. 'Even if it is not dishonest to identify ourselves with the tax collector, it isn't healthy. You seem to want us to wallow in sin.' On the contrary, evangelical Christians who take the subject of sin seriously and want to be faithful to the biblical doctrines of sin and salvation

are only being realists. Sin is serious, according to the Bible, because it is the assertion of self against God, our Creator, Lord and Judge, and against our neighbour whom we are meant to love and serve. And if nothing could deal with sin but the death of God's Son, it must be really serious. It is the false prophets who 'dress the wound of my people as though it were not serious. "Peace, peace," they say, when there is no peace.'[42]

3. It is said to be *selfish*. That is, 'Talk about *sin* is morbid, talk about *salvation* is selfish,' people say. 'You Christians are only interested in saving your own skins.'

This objection is so shallow that it hardly deserves comment. Christians who have received salvation by the mercy of God find themselves in the grip of Christ's love, with no alternative but to spend the rest of their lives in the service of God and their fellow human beings.

4. It is said to be *unjust*. 'Salvation by mercy alone, irrespective of any merit, simply isn't fair. The Pharisee was righteous. The tax collector *was* a sinner and it is outrageous that Jesus declared him righteous when he wasn't. It is a miscarriage of justice.'

But the Pharisee was only righteous outwardly, as we have already seen. Below the surface he was just as much a sinner as the tax collector. Both of them were sinners. Neither had loved God with all his being or his neighbour as himself. Yet only one faced up to the truth about himself and cried to God for mercy.

The truth is that if you really want justice, then both men, indeed all people, must be condemned. Only by the sin-bearing death of Christ has God provided a basis upon which he can declare the unrighteous righteous without compromising his own righteousness. Because of the cross God is able to 'demonstrate his righteousness at the present time, so as to be just and the one who justifies [i.e. declares righteous] those who have faith in Jesus'.[43] To receive what we deserve would mean condemnation; God offers us what Jesus Christ deserves and passes on to us – justification.

5. It is said to *undermine morality*. 'Evangelical doctrine is extremely dangerous,' our critics say. 'If sinners can be saved without any reference to who they are and what they do, the chief motivation for godly living is removed. Sin is encouraged, and social progress is hindered.'

The argument is as old as Paul's day. If salvation is by grace alone without merit, why don't we 'go on sinning so that grace may increase?'[44] Paul's answer to it, as convincing today as it was then, is that salvation involves union with Christ. It is 'in Christ' that God accepts us. And if anyone is in Christ, the new creation has come: the old life is finished, and a new life has begun. To put it another way, this union with Christ, brought about by God through faith and sealed in baptism, is particularly a union with him in his death and resurrection. His death was a death to sin – so since we are those who have died to sin, how can we live in it any longer?[45] The idea is a complete contradiction! And resurrection brought Christ into 'newness of life' in which we must live as well, since we have been spiritually raised with him. Indeed, once we have grasped what has happened to us through our union with Christ, we shall constantly 'count ourselves dead to sin but alive to God in Christ Jesus' and live accordingly.

The upshot of all this is that, although we cannot be saved by our good works, we also cannot be saved without them. Good works are not the route to salvation – but they are the necessary evidence that it has been received. The apostle James insists that faith which is not accompanied by action is dead. Such faith is not real or living or saving faith at all. The language of genuine faith is: 'I will show you my faith by my deeds.'[46] In Paul's words, it is 'faith expressing itself through love'.[47] So Paul and James do not contradict each other, as is sometimes claimed. It is only their emphasis which differs. Paul stresses the faith which leads to deeds, James the deeds which come from faith.

6. It is said to be *inhuman*, to demean humanity. 'Evangelical doctrine is insulting,' some say. 'It portrays human beings as feebly giving up the struggle, and looking helplessly for someone else to step in and do what we ought to be doing by ourselves. Surely, at the very least, we co-operate in our own salvation by choosing Christ?'

But Jesus himself was quite clear that the people he had come to seek and save were 'lost' – which is why he had come to seek and to save them. As Paul was to write later, if our acceptance with God could be achieved by our own obedience to the law, then 'Christ died for nothing!'[48] To suggest this is to insult Christ, which would be worse even than insulting humanity.

But the doctrine of human inability and of free and undeserved mercy is not an insult. It has been suggested that to speak of humanity's 'total depravity' goes too far and means the complete destruction of the image of God in human nature. But this is a mistaken criticism. No biblical Christian can deny that we are still 'made in the likeness of God', since this is what James clearly says we are.[49] The divine image in humanity is marred, but it is not destroyed. It is, however, marred at every point. That is the meaning of 'total depravity' – 'total' refers to extent rather than degree. So we happily affirm that human beings still bear the image of God, though we have to say that it is defaced, and we joyfully affirm that the image is restored in the new birth.[50] But we firmly deny that we can achieve our own salvation or even contribute to it. This may be humbling but it is a fact.

All six of the objections we have looked at are, in reality, ways of avoiding uncomfortable truths. The real reason why the doctrine of justification by grace alone through faith alone is unpopular is that it wounds our pride. It removes any ground for boasting. 'Where, then, is boasting? It is excluded.'[51] Instead, 'Let the one who boasts boast in the Lord.'[52] The gospel of free grace forces us to admit that we are 'poor in spirit', spiritually bankrupt, totally unable to purchase our own salvation, indeed 'wretched, pitiful, poor, blind and naked'.[53] It places us just where we do not want to be, beside the outcast tax collector, crying, 'God, have mercy on me, a sinner.'

Yet we cannot escape this stumbling-block, for it is central to biblical Christianity. The German Reformer Martin Luther was right to call justification by faith 'the principal article of all Christian doctrine, which maketh true Christians indeed'.[54] And the English Archbishop Thomas Cranmer endorsed it: 'This faith the Holy Scripture teacheth; this is the solid rock and foundation of Christian religion.'[55]

This great evangelical principle of a free salvation, illustrated by Christ in his parable and recovered from oblivion at the Reformation, is again largely ignored in the church. Lip-service is paid to it, but it is seldom preached. Yet it is both basic and distinctive to Christianity. All the other religions of the world are essentially systems of human merit. Even those which teach the mercy of God emphasize that his mercy has to be earned. Only Christianity announces that God is merciful to sinners who do not deserve his mercy. They are those who have only the merit of Christ to plead, and whose only argument is the humble, believing cry, 'God, be merciful to me, a sinner!'

5

Morality:
Outward or inward?

So far we have considered four major topics of controversy between Jesus Christ and the Jewish leaders of his day: religion, authority, Scripture and salvation. We have seen how, in opposition to the Pharisees and Sadducees, Jesus taught:

- that religion is not natural but supernatural (a life lived by the power of God),
- that authority is not in tradition but in Scripture (because tradition is human while Scripture is divine),
- that Scripture is not an end in itself but a means to an end (pointing us to Christ that we may find life in Christ),
- and that salvation is due not to human merit but to God's mercy.

The fifth topic of controversy is morality. Logically it comes next, because in a sense it is part of salvation, since 'salvation' includes holiness of life as well as acceptance with God, sanctification as well as justification. What, then, is the nature of the good life? And how can we achieve it? In any given situation how can we know which action would be right and which wrong? What is it that makes us clean or unclean in God's sight?

Old and new views of right and wrong

These are important questions, and the answers given by the Pharisees differed widely from those given by Jesus Christ. They are still a field of controversy today and so we shall seek to discover if Christ's discussion with the Pharisees throws any light on the contemporary debate.

First, some definitions and explanations. The traditional way of thinking about right and wrong is commonly called 'prescriptive', because in it the rules are largely laid down before you begin, whereas a more modern approach is called 'situational' because (according to this way of thinking) it is the situation itself, not any pre-set rules, which should guide your behaviour. The advocates of situational morality reject the old for two principal reasons. First, because it is *authoritarian*. It is a morality revealed in divine laws and reinforced by divine sanctions. Right conduct is imposed by an external authority called 'God'. A situational ethic, on the other hand, is said to need no authority but its own intrinsic reasonableness.

Secondly, they reject it because it is *absolute*. Laws are inflexible things, they argue, and life is too complicated to be governed by rigid rules. The new morality, on the other hand, is guided by love, and love can adapt itself to each situation in a way that law cannot.

Those who hold this approach take it further. They go on to claim both Jesus Christ and the apostle Paul as its champions. They maintain that Jesus himself out of love broke the law on a number of occasions, especially with regard to the Sabbath.

And they like to quote some of Paul's sayings such as 'we are not under the law' or 'Christ is the end of the law' or 'love is the fulfilling of the law'. Believing that they have both Jesus and Paul on their side, they are happy to do away altogether with the category of law in Christian ethics.

Only one point needs to be made at this stage, namely that the life and teaching of Jesus do not demonstrate such a neat distinction between law and love. The contrast they pose is a false one. We are being forced to make a choice which the Bible neither makes itself nor asks us to make. It's certainly the case that Jesus made love the top priority. This is common ground. But in doing so he did not reject law. What he rejected were *misinterpretations* of the law, not the law itself. On the contrary, he obeyed it in his own life. He stated clearly that he had come not to abolish the law, but to fulfil it. He also boldly echoed God's word in Exodus 20:6 ('those who love me and keep my commandments') by insisting that his disciples must love him and keep his commandments.

The Pharisees' obsession

One mistake we need to guard against is the failure to distinguish between 'law' and 'legalism'. Legalism is a wrong use of law, by which it is distorted – either into a way of salvation or a mere code of outward behaviour. What Jesus rejected was the legalism of the Pharisees, not the law of Moses revealed by God. His opposition to the morality of the Pharisees was not that their view of the law was authoritarian (imposed from above), nor that it was absolute (and therefore inflexible), but that it was external. In practice, they were reducing the law's absolute and authoritative demands. They were attempting to make the law less daunting and more manageable by putting it into a neat set of man-made rules. As a result, their obedience was only skin-deep and not from the heart, which is what primarily concerns God.

Let us look at Mark's record of the controversy:[1]

The Pharisees and some of the teachers of the law who had come from Jerusalem gathered around Jesus and saw some of his disciples eating food with hands that were defiled, that is, unwashed. (The Pharisees and all the Jews do not eat unless they give their hands a ceremonial washing, holding to the tradition of the elders. When they come from the market-place they do not eat unless they wash. And they observe many other traditions, such as the washing of cups, pitchers and kettles.)

So the Pharisees and teachers of the law asked Jesus, 'Why don't your disciples live according to the tradition of the elders instead of eating their food with defiled hands?'

He replied, 'Isaiah was right when he prophesied about you hypocrites; as it is written:

"These people honour me with their lips,
    but their hearts are far from me.
They worship me in vain;
    their teachings are merely human rules."

'You have let go of the commands of God and are holding on to human traditions . . .'

Again Jesus called the crowd to him and said, 'Listen to me, everyone, and understand this. Nothing outside a person can defile them by going into them. Rather, it is what comes out of a person that defiles them.'

After he had left the crowd and entered the house, his disciples asked him about this parable. 'Are you so dull?' he asked. 'Don't you see that nothing that enters a person from the outside can defile them? For it doesn't go into their heart but into their stomach, and then out of the body.' (In saying this, Jesus declared all foods clean.)

He went on: 'What comes out of a person is what defiles them. For it is from within, out of a person's heart, that evil thoughts come – sexual immorality, theft, murder, adultery, greed, malice, deceit, lewdness, envy, slander, arrogance and folly. All these evils come from inside and defile a person.'

We began to study this passage in chapter 2, in order to illustrate our Lord's view of the relation between Scripture and tradition. The occasion of the controversy was that the Pharisees saw some of Jesus' disciples, perhaps on their return from the market-place (6:56), eating 'with hands that were defiled, that is, unwashed' (vv. 1, 2). Mark goes on to explain to his Gentile readers (vv. 3, 4) that the Pharisees – and indeed 'all the Jews', following popular Pharisaic teaching – were scrupulous in 'holding to the tradition of the elders', particularly in the matter of purifying themselves by washing their hands before eating, and by washing cups, pitchers and kettles as well. After this explanation Mark continues his narrative. The Pharisees came to Jesus and asked (v. 5), 'Why don't your disciples live according to the tradition of the elders instead of eating their food with defiled hands?' It is important to note that two separate questions were combined here. The first was general as to why the disciples of Jesus did not conform to the ancient traditions; the second concerned a particular tradition regarding purification and why the disciples did not observe it.

Jesus goes on to answer both questions. He begins by quoting Isaiah 29:13 as a prophecy referring to the Pharisees, in which the two subjects are touched upon. God roundly rebukes his Pharisaic people both for their worship (which is a merely a matter of what they say and not from the heart) and for their teaching (which is all about human traditions of men rather than the commands of God). Basing what he says on this Old Testament verse, Jesus proceeds to explain and illustrate this double theme. First, he speaks about the place of tradition, and secondly, about the nature of defilement and therefore of purification. First (in vv. 6–13) he places tradition in second place to Scripture, as we saw in chapter 2. Secondly (in vv. 14–23) he insists that the defilement and therefore the purification which really matter are inward and moral, not outward and ritual. What defiles people in God's sight is not the food which enters their stomach, but the sin which comes out of their heart.

The portrait of the Pharisees which Mark paints here is accurate and fair. These Pharisees of the first century AD were descended from the *Hasidim* ('pious people') of a century or two earlier. The word 'Pharisees' means 'separated ones', and was applied to them 'when they withdrew from the Sadducee court party of the Maccabean rulers and John Hyrcanus (135–105 BC)'.[2] They were determined to resist the incoming tide of Greek influence. Fundamental to their position was this principle, that they 'regarded nature and spirit as so related that impurity could pass from one to the other'. Thus, 'a bad man's body was impure, and to touch it would bring uncleanness to another man's soul.'[3] This principle naturally led them to devise complicated ritual regulations, which were later collected in the six divisions of the Mishnah. Their aim was to be as ceremonially pure in daily life as the priests were in the temple.

High on the list of these rules about ceremonial purification was the matter of hand-washing. 'He who lightly esteems hand-washing,' went one tradition, 'will perish from the earth.' This emphasis was universal among them. The commentator Edersheim describes how strictly the rituals were observed. He points out that the rabbis Hillel and Shammai, the two great rival teachers who flourished shortly before Christ, disagreed on many points. But they were united in what they said about the regulations to do with hand-washing and on the 'eighteen decrees' which were intended to purify the Jews from defiling contact with Gentiles.[4]

It is little wonder, therefore, that when they saw the disciples of Jesus eat without washing their hands, and heard his teaching about it, 'the Pharisees were offended'.[5]

So what did Jesus say? The next paragraph (vv. 14–23) is divided into two parts, the first being what he said to the crowd, and the second to the disciples. To the crowd he said, 'Listen to me, everyone, and understand this. Nothing outside a person can defile them by going into them. Rather, it is what comes out of a person that defiles them' (vv. 14, 15). In saying this, he establishes the fundamental principle: what defiles a person, rendering them unclean in the sight of God, is what comes out of them, not what goes into them. Jesus goes into this in more detail with his disciples later when they're on their own (vv. 17–23). In answer to a question they asked him, he first expresses his disappointment that their understanding is no greater than that of the crowd. Then he goes on: 'Don't you see that nothing that enters a person from the outside can defile them?' whereas 'What comes out of a person is what defiles them.' Away from the crowd, Jesus now expands on this contrast between what 'enters' and what 'comes out' with the disciples. What 'goes in' is food. It cannot defile because (v. 19) 'it doesn't go into their heart but into their stomach, and then out of the body'. Mark adds that 'in saying this, Jesus declared all foods clean', effectively setting aside the Old Testament food regulations. What 'comes out', on the other hand, is sin. This is what defiles a person, because it comes from their heart (vv. 20, 21).

There follows an ugly catalogue of thirteen evils. The first, which seems to be general and to cover the rest, is 'evil thoughts'. Perhaps Christ was thinking of the hostile thoughts which the Pharisees were harbouring about him at the very moment when they were expressing their concern about proper purification. Next come six words in the plural, indicating repeated acts of sin, followed by six words in the singular, emphasizing the sinful state or act itself. 'All these,' Jesus concluded, are 'evils' which 'come from inside and defile a person' (v. 23). This sentence contains an important twofold statement about the origin and outcome of sin, the cause and effect of all human wrongdoing. Its origin is the heart, and its outcome defilement in the sight of God.

Having looked briefly at Christ's answer to the disciples' question, we must reflect on its implications. In general, the Pharisees were obsessed with external, ritual purification – clean hands, clean foods, clean vessels. Jesus, on the other hand, stressed the essential inwardness of morality, that God's concern is more with the heart than with the hands.

From these verses, and from other disputes which Jesus had with the Pharisees over morality, we may draw four implications. They can be expressed in four statements.

1. The new birth is indispensable

It's true that Jesus does not mention the new birth as such in this passage. But the evangelical insistence upon regeneration or new birth arises directly from what he teaches here. Since the heart is the source of the 'evils' people do and say, a change in behaviour requires a change of heart.

It is difficult to understand those who still cling to the idea that human nature is fundamentally good, especially in the light of all the evil that is in the world today. It is even harder to understand those who claim that this is what Jesus thought, when the fact is that he taught nothing of the kind. This question is so important that we must investigate it more deeply. What did Jesus think and say about human nature?

The first thing to be said is that he taught the essential dignity of humanity. Although he is never recorded as having used the expression, there can be no doubt that he accepted what the Old Testament says about God making human beings in his own image and endowing them with capacities – rational, moral, social and spiritual – which distinguish them from animals. And despite human fallenness and sinfulness (to which we shall come in a moment), Jesus evidently thought that human beings still retained a residue of their former glory. So he spoke clearly of human value – a human being is 'worth more than many sparrows',[6] for example. And the clearest evidence he gave of the value he placed on human beings was his own mission, which he undertook solely for humanity's benefit. Like a shepherd who, having lost a single sheep, first misses it and then braves hardship and danger to rescue it, so God misses human beings who get lost and sent Jesus Christ as the Good Shepherd to seek and to save them. Indeed, his search for straying sheep would take him to the cross. 'The good shepherd lays down his life for the sheep.'[7] Nothing reveals more clearly how precious we are to God and the depth of his love for us than the death of God's Son for our salvation.

But alongside his teaching on the essential dignity of human beings, Christ also taught about the depths to which we have sunk. The Old Testament had taught that 'there is no one who does good, not even one',[8] a view which Jesus fully agreed with. On two or three occasions he referred to his contemporaries as a 'wicked and adulterous generation'[9] – 'wicked' because of their unbelief and disobedience, 'adulterous' because they had transferred their love and loyalty from the living God to idols of their own making.

Nor was he just passing judgment on his own generation; he was referring to humanity as a whole. In the Sermon on the Mount he said, 'If you, then, though you are evil, know how to give good gifts to your children, how much more will your Father in heaven give good gifts to those who ask him!'[10] This statement is particularly striking because it freely concedes that fallen men and women can give 'good' gifts. It is perfectly true that parents love their children, make sacrifices on their behalf and give them good gifts. But they are still labelled as 'evil'. In other words, even when we see people at their very best, following the finest instincts of parenthood, Jesus still calls them 'evil'.

Jesus confirmed his view of human sin and corruption with all that he taught about our lostness and sickness. His vivid pictures of the shepherd seeking the lost sheep and the doctor healing the sick tell us both about the hopeless state we are in and also about how precious we are to the God who loves us.

It is especially clear in his controversy with the Pharisees over defilement. Let us look closely at what he says in this passage by giving a literal translation of the Greek of verses 20–23: 'What comes out of *the man*, that defiles *the man*. For from inside, out of the heart of *the men* their evil thoughts come out . . . All these evil things come out from inside and defile *the man*.' Notice the repeated use of the definite article. Jesus Christ was not painting a portrait of one particular evil-doer, but of every human being. He was speaking about people who were cultured, refined, moral and religious – the Pharisees on the one hand and his own disciples on the other!

Jesus taught that within the soil of every human heart there lie buried the ugly seeds of every imaginable sin – 'evil thoughts, sexual immorality, theft, murder, adultery, greed, malice, deceit, lewdness, envy, slander, arrogance and folly'. All thirteen are 'evils', and they come out of the heart of every person. This is Jesus Christ's assessment of fallen human nature.

So then, according to Jesus, the 'evils' which we think, say and do are not due primarily to our environment, nor are they bad habits picked up from bad teaching, bad company or bad example; they are due to the inward corruption of our heart. This is not to say that environment, education and example are unimportant. No, their influence for good or bad is very strong, and Christians should set themselves in these areas to encourage the good and eliminate the bad. What we are saying (because Jesus said it long ago) is that the dominant force in a person's life is the nature they are born with, and that the ultimate origin of evil thoughts and deeds is the evil heart, which is by nature twisted with self-centredness. As God had said through the prophet Jeremiah centuries earlier, 'The heart is deceitful above all things and beyond cure. Who can understand it?'[11]

Our Lord's favourite way of illustrating that our words and deeds are governed by our heart was that of the tree and its fruit. 'By their fruit you will recognize them,' he said of false prophets. And more elaborately: 'every good tree bears good fruit, but a bad tree bears bad fruit. A good tree cannot bear bad fruit, and a bad tree cannot bear good fruit . . . Thus, by their fruit you will recognize them.'[12] We do not have to guess what he meant by this, because he spelled it out elsewhere. The tree is a person's heart or nature, and the fruit their words and deeds. As the condition of a tree determines the fruit it bears, so a person's heart determines their behaviour. Thus, 'How can you who are evil say anything good? For the mouth speaks what the heart is full of.'[13] We say and do evil things because we have an evil heart or nature; it is from inside, out of our heart, that evil things and evil thoughts arise.

Psychoanalysis has tended only to confirm this teaching of the Old Testament endorsed by Jesus, because it has further uncovered the horrid secrets of the human heart. Both psychology and experience tell us that the subconscious mind (which is more or less equivalent to what the Bible means by 'heart', namely the centre of our personality, the source of our thoughts and emotions) is like a deep well with a thick deposit of mud at the bottom. Normally, being at the bottom, the mud is safely out of sight. But when the waters of the well are stirred, especially by the currents of violent emotion, the most evil-looking and evil-smelling filth breaks the surface – rage, spite, greed, lust, jealousy, malice, cruelty and revenge. These base passions keep bubbling up, raw and sinister, from the secret springs of the heart. And if we have any moral sensitivity, we must at times be appalled, shocked and disgusted by the foul things which lurk in the hidden depths of our personality.

The conclusion which Christ draws from this principle (the principle that our heart controls our hands, or our nature governs our behaviour) is that only a 'radical' solution will do – a solution which goes to the root (*radix*) of the problem. Since the heart of the problem is the heart, good behaviour depends on our being given a new heart. Which is exactly what Jesus said was possible: 'Make a tree good and its fruit will be good.'[14] Do this and this will happen: 'A good man brings good things out of the good stored up in his heart.'[15]

Jesus spelled this out further in his conversation with Nicodemus set out in chapter 3 of John's Gospel. Nicodemus was a Pharisee, who represents the very best that Pharisaism could produce. He does not seem to have suffered from the hypocrisy that wrecked so much of the Pharisees' religion. On the contrary, he appears to have been a sincere and humble seeker after the truth. Yet it was to him that Jesus said, 'Very truly I tell you, no one can see the kingdom of God unless they are born again . . . Flesh gives birth to flesh, but the Spirit gives birth to spirit. You should not be surprised at my saying, "You must be born again"' (vv. 3, 6, 7). The word he used in connection with this new birth was the Greek word *anōthen*, an adverb that could equally well mean 'from the beginning, again, anew' or 'from above' (like the Temple curtain which was torn in half 'from top' to bottom).[16] It's likely that Jesus deliberately chose a word with two meanings in order to underline the truth that the new birth is both a *second* birth and a *divine* birth, both a fresh beginning and a miracle of God. To be 'born again' (vv. 3, 7) is to be 'born of the Spirit' (vv. 5, 8). So the new birth is a profound inward change, the planting by God of a new life, the gift of a new nature, the donation of a new heart. Though it could be and was experienced in Old Testament times, the Old Testament points to it as one of the greatest blessings which the New Covenant will bring: 'I will give you a new heart and put a new spirit in you . . . I will put my Spirit in you and move you to follow my decrees and be careful to keep my laws . . .'[17] Again, 'I will put my law in their minds and write it on their hearts.'[18]

In this new birth, and in the new life which then begins, the work of the Holy Spirit is crucial. It is the Spirit who brings about new birth or regeneration. It is the Spirit also who indwells every born-again believer and sanctifies them. This is why Paul refers to holiness as 'the fruit of the Spirit'. Perhaps he is echoing Christ's own teaching about trees and their fruit. At all events, the nine beautiful graces he lists – 'love, joy, peace, forbearance, kindness, goodness, faithfulness, gentleness and self-control'[19] – are qualities which the Holy Spirit himself produces, cultivating them in a Christian's character as in an orchard.

So the Christian should be like a fruit tree, not a Christmas tree! For the gaudy decorations of a Christmas tree are only *tied* on, whereas fruit *grows* on a fruit tree. In other words, Christian holiness is not an artificial human addition, but a natural process of fruit-bearing by the power of the Holy Spirit. As Jesus was later to promise his apostles in the Upper Room: 'I am the vine; you are the branches. If you remain in me and I in you, you will bear much fruit; apart from me you can do nothing.'[20]

These great doctrines – the necessity of the new birth for a new life and the work of the Holy Spirit in both regeneration and sanctification – are true evangelical emphases. They are part and parcel of Christ's teaching about the essential inwardness of both evil and morality. J. C. Ryle, Bishop of Liverpool in the nineteenth century, put it like this:

> We hold that a mighty spiritual disease like this requires a mighty spiritual medicine for its cure ... We dread fostering man's favourite notion that a little church-going and sacrament-receiving – a little patching, and mending, and whitewashing, and gilding, and polishing, and varnishing, and painting the outside – is all that his case requires ... It requires nothing less than ... the grace of God the Holy Ghost entirely renewing the heart ... I believe that ignorance of the extent of the fall, and of the whole doctrine of original sin, is one grand reason why many can neither understand, appreciate nor receive Evangelical Religion. Next to the Bible, as its foundation, it is based on a clear view of original sin.[21]

It seems right at this point to add a word of caution, even of evangelical self-criticism and penitence. Our right emphasis on the need for new birth and on the impossibility of true holiness without it has sometimes led evangelicals down a wrong path. This is best described as 'pietism'. Historically, the word has been used to describe various tendencies, both good and bad. I am using it here, for want of a better term, to refer to that kind of personal devotion which results in a withdrawal from social and even moral responsibility. The kind of 'pietistic' position I have in mind might be argued in this way: 'If goodness is the fruit of the Spirit, the natural product of a heart renewed and inhabited by the Spirit, then this and nothing else really matters. There is no need to teach Christians how to behave, for it will come to them naturally. Furthermore, there is no point in trying to promote morality in unrenewed people or to bring about better social structures, since moral and social renewal are the automatic consequence of personal renewal and cannot take place without it.'

I do not think this overstates the case. Evangelical Christians have undoubtedly thought and spoken like this from time to time. Indeed, I have done so myself. But this point of view is a false deduction from a true doctrine. The new birth is vital, indeed essential, for entry into God's kingdom and for Christ-likeness. But it is not the be-all and end-all of Christian life and responsibility. We have other duties to both the renewed and the unrenewed, that is, to both Christians and non-Christians.

Take Christians first. To say that sanctification is a *natural* consequence of regeneration does not mean that it is an *auto-matic* consequence. Even though born again, a Christian can still behave badly and thoughtlessly, sin grievously, fail in personal relationships and face other problems. This is evident from the New Testament and in the lives of our fellow-Christians, yes, and we know it in our own lives also. This is why such detailed instructions are set out in the Epistles – about controlling the tongue, about the duty of working hard to earn our living, about being honest, just, hospitable, forgiving and kind, about sexual purity, and about the relationships between husbands and wives, parents and children, masters and servants. But surely these were Christian people, born-again people? Yes, they were! But the apostles did not take the holiness of their readers for granted; they worked for it by detailed instruction, by exhortation, example and prayer.

What then about the non-Christian? Here too we have a Christian responsibility. It would be wrong to argue that, since the key to morality and justice is the new birth, and since social renewal depends on personal renewal, it is useless either to teach righteousness to non-Christians or to concern ourselves with the structures of society. We have no right to say that our sole responsibility as Christians is to preach the gospel of salvation, on the grounds that moral and social righteousness will then follow naturally.

I say we do not have this right simply because the Bible itself does not grant it to us. If, therefore, we concentrate exclusively on personal conversion and personal morality, we are not being true to our claim to be biblical Christians. We need to remember that the living God of the Bible is not only the Saviour and Father of his covenant people; he is also the Creator, Lord and Judge of all humanity. And he is a righteous God who loves righteousness, who is concerned (as the prophet Amos showed)[22] for the practice of righteousness and for the punishment of unrighteousness in every human community, in all the nations, not just Israel and Judah. Similarly, Christian parents are to bring up their children 'in the training and instruction of the Lord'[23] right from the start. They should not wait until their children profess their own Christian faith before teaching them about right and wrong. Again, the God-given function of every state, however secular and godless it may be, is to punish those who do wrong in order to restrain evil and promote good in the whole community, whether Christian or not.[24] Furthermore, although individuals have – or can have – more influence on their environment than their environment has on them, and although it is more our heredity than our environment which makes all of us what we are, this is no excuse for being callously indifferent to what is going on in the world around us. For people are profoundly affected by their environment (whether by 'environment' we are thinking of political tyranny, social injustice, racial discrimination, unemployment, poverty, bad housing, undernourishment or an inadequate health service). Besides, even if people were not adversely affected by a bad environment, it would still be right to play our part in the attempt to improve it. Whether or not such efforts are successful, simple justice and love demand that we at least try to do our bit. In other words, Christians should aim to be good citizens as well as a good witnesses. If we are spreading the good news of salvation through Jesus Christ, of a new birth and a new life, we should also be joining in the fight against social injustice and political oppression, and so contribute, however little, to the search for a social order which guarantees freedom, justice, dignity and welfare for all people.

2. God looks on the heart

A second conclusion which may be drawn from Christ's controversy with the Pharisees over morality is that God's primary concern is with the condition of a person's heart. 'For it is from within,' he insisted, 'out of a person's heart, that evil thoughts come . . . All these evils come from inside and defile a person.' Again, 'God knows your hearts.'[25]

In fact, several of the 'evils' Christ listed not only come out of the heart, but also remain in the heart as inward and secret offences. Thus, 'evil thoughts' may break out in evil words or deeds, but they are still evil even if they never erupt visibly. 'Covetousness' may or may not lead to theft, but it is still evil even when it never gets further than our thoughts and desires. Similarly, 'pride' usually betrays its presence in arrogance and vanity, but even if someone who is proud manages to look humble, their secret pride is still detestable in God's sight. So the wrong desires of the heart, in the apostle John's language 'the lusts of the flesh', are themselves evil from God's point of view, quite apart from the sins of speech and action to which they frequently lead.

This is what lies behind the astonishing statement which Jesus made to his disciples in the Sermon on the Mount, namely that 'unless your righteousness surpasses that of the Pharisees and the teachers of the law, you will certainly not enter the kingdom of heaven'.[26] Now the Pharisees were, in their own way, very righteous indeed. They calculated that the law contained 248 commandments and 365 prohibitions, and they were meticulous in observing them all (at least outwardly). When it came to keeping the law they could say, as did Saul the Pharisee, that they were 'faultless'.[27]

How then could Jesus insist that the righteousness of his disciples must surpass the righteousness of the Pharisees, and warn them that, if it did not, they would never enter God's kingdom? The answer is not difficult to find. Despite the Pharisees' enthusiasm for righteousness, their view of it was shallow. They concentrated their attention on an outward conformity to the law (as they understood it) and imagined that this was enough. They also embellished it with their traditional interpretations.

But in the Sermon on the Mount Jesus taught that God's standards were much higher and his analysis much deeper than the Pharisees ever realized. He went on (Matthew 5:21–48) to utter six parallel instructions, each introduced by the same formula, 'You have heard that it was said . . . But I tell you . . . '

Some think that Jesus was introducing a new law, and that in doing so he was contradicting and cancelling the old. Nothing could be further from the truth. Not only would this run counter to his lifelong attitude of reverent assent to Scripture, but he had just made clear that he had not 'come to abolish the law and the prophets . . . but to fulfil them' (v. 17). He then solemnly added that 'until heaven and earth disappear, not the smallest letter, not the least stroke of a pen, will by any means disappear from the Law until everything is accomplished' (v. 18), and warned his hearers that anybody who 'sets aside one of the least of these commands and teaches others accordingly will be called least in the kingdom of heaven' (v. 19). In the light of these statements it is absurd to suggest that Jesus was disagreeing with the law.

No. What Jesus was contradicting here was not Scripture but tradition, not what 'is written' but what 'was said', not God's Word but the false interpretations of it which the teachers of the law and Pharisees were guilty of. In each case they were attempting to reduce the challenge of the divine law in order to suit their convenience, either by restricting what it commanded or by extending what it permitted. This is why Jesus said that the righteousness of Christian disciples must surpass the righteousness of Pharisees. The Pharisees were tampering with the law to make it less demanding; the disciple must accept its full force and all its implications.

Take what the law allowed, which the traditions of the elders sought to extend. The law permitted divorce when a husband found 'some indecency' in his wife. But tradition was increasingly extending this permission to include any arbitrary whim of a husband. The Pharisees asked, 'Is it lawful for a man to divorce his wife for any and every reason?' In his answer Jesus referred them back to what Genesis says about the lifelong purpose of marriage, and then seems to have restricted the grounds for divorce to sexual unfaithfulness.[28] Again, the law permitted retribution in the courts, in order to guide the magistrate and to restrict penalties to this maximum or to some equivalent restitution ('eye for eye, and tooth for tooth').[29] Traditional interpretation, however, seems to have extended this permission to the area of personal relationships and to have used it to justify personal revenge. Jesus insisted that this was a perverse manipulation of the law, and that the Christian way was to accept a personal injustice without resisting and without seeking revenge.[30]

The teachers of the law not only attempted to extend the law's permissions; they also tried to restrict the law's uncomfortable commands. For example, God's law said 'love your neighbour'. Tradition interpreted the word 'neighbour' narrowly, applying it only to a fellow-Israelite, or even simply to a friend. In so doing the teachers of the law were effectively distorting the command 'love your neighbour' into 'love your neighbour *and hate your enemy*' (which, of course, the law says nowhere). Jesus flatly contradicted this tradition and taught instead that, properly understood, our neighbour *includes* our enemy: 'But I tell you, love your enemies . . . '[31] Similarly, the teachers of the law restricted the command, 'Do not break your oath, but fulfil to the Lord the vows you have made' as if it prohibited some oaths but permitted others. But Jesus accepted no such limitation. On the contrary, the true meaning of the command, he said, was 'do not swear an oath at all'. All promises must be kept, and the Christian disciple should be so truthful that he has no need to back up any promise with an oath. 'All you need to say is simply "Yes" or "No"; anything beyond this comes from the evil one.'[32]

The principle is the same with the other two commandments Jesus mentions here, those relating to murder and adultery. The traditions of the Jewish elders were much in line with the standards of today's world and restricted these prohibitions to the act alone. But Jesus emphasized that they had a much more searching application. The angry thought and the insulting word also breach the law against murder, he said, and put us at risk of judgment. Similarly, the lustful look is equivalent to adultery, for 'anyone who looks at a woman lustfully has already committed adultery with her *in his heart*'.[33]

These six illustrations leave us in no doubt what Jesus meant when he said that Christian righteousness must surpass Pharisaic righteousness. Christian righteousness accepts the full implications of the law without trying to dodge them. It recognizes that the law's authority extends beyond the actual deed to the word, and beyond the word to the thoughts and motives of the heart. Pharisaic righteousness was an outward conformity to human traditions; Christian righteousness is an inward conformity of mind and heart to the revealed will of God.

Much of the thinking about morality in our modern world has a similar (though not identical) tendency to that of Pharisaic morality. Not that its advocates think so, of course! They maintain that Jesus had a much more liberal attitude to the law than the Pharisees (witness their horrified reaction to his 'breaking' of the Sabbath law), and they go on to claim that what they are saying to the defenders of more traditional moral standards is no different from what Jesus was saying to the Pharisees. We do not believe, however, that Jesus either broke the Sabbath law or would even have dreamed of doing so (since he accepted its divine origin). What he did was to flout some of the traditions of the elders about the Sabbath – but in so doing he demonstrated the true intention of God's command. We shall come back to this later.

Of course there is a radical difference between the morality of the Pharisees and the approach to morality we find in today's world. The former was absolutist and prescriptive, while the latter is relativistic and situational. Even so, there is one point which they share. This is that both have the effect of toning down the law's demands. The Pharisees were guilty of misinterpreting the law, Jesus said, and so of reducing its challenge. Today our world goes further and insists that Christians shouldn't worry about 'law' at all. Apart, that is, from the all-embracing law of love. This is an absolute; there are no others. All morality is relative to the one and only absolute of love. Nothing else makes a thing right or wrong.

It is essential to be fair to those who adopt this position. They are not – at least the best of them are not – encouraging a complete free-for-all. Some of them even maintain that the demands of love are more rather than less rigorous than those of law. This is a doubtful claim, however. How could the demands of love alone be greater than the demands of both law and love together? And anyway, there can be no doubt that the popular understanding of morality based on love alone is that it is a lot less demanding. For example, even the prohibition against adultery may be ignored if the adulterer sincerely believes that their action is consistent with love.

The biblical Christian affirms that love and law are not incompatible with one another, let alone mutually exclusive. For love needs law to guide it. It is rather naïve to claim that love has no need of any direction outside itself because 'it has a built-in moral compass, enabling it to "home" intuitively upon the deepest need of the other'. What about the fact that human beings are fallen? Love is far from infallible. Indeed, it is sometimes blind! The reason God has given us commandments is to help us chart the pathways of love. Hence Paul's statement: 'whoever loves others has fulfilled the law. The commandments, "You shall not commit adultery," "You shall not murder," "You shall not steal," "You shall not covet," and whatever other command there may be, are summed up in this one command: "Love your neighbour as yourself." Love does no harm to a neighbour. Therefore love is the fulfilment of the law.'[34] Love is not the *finish* of the law (in the sense that it dispenses with it); love is the *fulfilment* of the law (in the sense that it obeys it). What the New Testament says about law and love is not 'if you love you can break the law', but 'if you love you will keep it'.

Why, then, does Paul say that Christians are 'not under law'? It is true that he uses this expression several times, but never on its own. He always supplies (or at least implies) a contrast. The fact is that we can never understand the meaning of a negative unless we know with what it is being contrasted. For example, if I simply wrote of someone that 'he does not behave like a man', you would not know if I was being extremely complimentary and implying that he was more like an angel, or if I was being rude and implying that he was more like a child. I remember once, on my return from a trip to America and Australia, that I shocked my friends by saying, 'I haven't had a bath for seven weeks.' Before they had time to take me to task for my un-hygienic habits, however, I was able to add, 'But I've had a shower every day!' Negatives are misleading unless they are read in the light of the positives with which they are being contrasted.

Now Paul never expressed his negatives in isolation. When he says that Christians are 'not under law', he never meant that the category of law has been altogether abolished, but rather that we do not look to the law for either our justification or our sanctification. It would in any case be useless for us to do so, because of the law's 'weakness'. Paul writes: '[God did] what the law was powerless to do because it was *weakened by the flesh*.'[35] It is clear from this that the problem is not with the law but with us. Because of our fallen nature, we cannot by ourselves keep the law. And because we cannot keep the law, it can neither justify nor sanctify us. Instead, God has done for us and in us what the law is powerless to do. And he has done it by the sending of both his Son and his Spirit. He justifies us through the death of his Son and sanctifies us through the indwelling of his Spirit. That is to say, God accepts us, not because we strive to obey the law, but because of the finished work of Christ. And our route to holiness is not through our efforts to obey the law but through the inward work of the Spirit.

It is in this double sense, then, that Paul declares we have been 'freed' from the law and urges us to stand firm in the freedom with which Christ has set us free. It is in this sense too that he tells us we are 'not under the law'. We are now able to understand his negative from its positive counterparts. As for our justification: 'You are not under the law, but under grace.'[36] As for our sanctification: 'if you are led by the Spirit you are not under the law.'[37] What he is saying is that our justification depends not on law but on grace, and our sanctification not on law but on the Spirit. Christian believers don't rely on the law for their justification and their sanctification; instead they rely on God's grace for both. For 'law' is all about own efforts at obedience, whereas 'grace' means God's plan to save us through his Son and his Spirit.

But the fact that the law is unable to provide us with the ground of our justification or the means of our sanctification does not mean that we can dispense with it altogether. We still need it as a guide to how we should behave. Even though we are justified by grace rather than law, God justifies us 'in order that the righteous requirement of the law might be fully met in us . . .'[38] Again, even though we are sanctified by the Spirit rather than law, what the Spirit does in sanctifying us is precisely to write the law in our hearts![39] Keeping God's law is not the *basis* on which we are put right with God – but it is the *result* of it. Again, keeping God's law is not the *means* of our sanctification – but it is the *essence* of it. The Puritan Samuel Bolton summed up Paul's teaching about the law and the gospel like this: 'The law sends us to the Gospel, that we may be justified, and the Gospel sends us to the law again to enquire what is our duty being justified.'[40]

So when in one place Paul writes that 'neither circumcision nor uncircumcision means anything; what counts is the new creation'[41] and in another place 'circumcision is nothing and uncircumcision is nothing. Keeping God's commands is what counts',[42] he is not contradicting himself. For a new enthusiasm to keep God's commandments is exactly what the new creation (or new birth) leads to. Indeed, John insists that 'sin is lawlessness',[43] while one of the important evidences of the new birth is that we do not persist in such sin but obey God's commandments instead.[44]

When the Holy Spirit writes God's law in our hearts, he gives us both an inward understanding of its meaning and a fervent desire to obey it. The language of the regenerate believer, with which the stance of the new morality cannot easily be reconciled, is 'Oh, how I love your law! I meditate on it all day long',[45] 'in my inner being I delight in God's law',[46] and 'the precepts of the Lord are right, giving joy to the heart'.[47]

All of which brings us back to the *heart* again, to the difference between Pharisaic righteousness and Christian righteousness, and to Christ's insistence that we keep God's law, not with a reluctant, external conformity, but with a willing, inward conformity of mind and will and heart.

3. The moral takes precedence over the ceremonial
The third implication which may be drawn from Christ's controversy with the Pharisees over morality concerns the comparative

importance of moral and ceremonial duties. The Pharisaic concept of both defilement and purification was largely a ritual one. They were rigorous about what they were allowed and not allowed to eat. In addition, the vessels in which the food was prepared, and from which it was later eaten, had first to be cleansed with faultless ceremonial precision. And they would never eat it with defiled (that is, unwashed) hands. Thus, foods, vessels and hands all had to be clean.

Now some of these laws were laws of God, which Jesus had no quarrel with. Other regulations belonged to 'the traditions of the elders' rather than Scripture. But there was nothing in Scripture to contradict them, so obeying them was optional. Yet by concentrating on such ceremonial matters, the Pharisees came to think of morality in these terms, largely as a matter of bodily purification. Hence Christ's emphasis that what defiles a person is what comes out from inside them, from the heart. For the purity God requires first of all is not ceremonial (clean foods, hands and vessels) but moral (a holy life).

Some striking examples of this principle occur in Matthew 23, in which Jesus pronounced a number of 'woes' upon the teachers of the law and Pharisees. 'Woe to you, teachers of the law and Pharisees, you hypocrites! You clean the outside of the cup and dish, but inside they are full of greed and self-indulgence. Blind Pharisee! First clean the inside of the cup and dish, and then the outside also will be clean' (vv. 25, 26). The Lord's complaint was that the Pharisees were so keen on getting the ritual cleansing of their cups and plates right that they were unconcerned about the food and drink contained in their ceremonially clean vessels being morally unclean through dishonesty and greed. They were blind to this inconsistency.

Again, 'Woe to you, teachers of the law and Pharisees, you hypocrites! You give a tenth of your spices – mint, dill and cumin [i.e. you are meticulous in giving God a tenth of even the smallest herbs you grow in your back garden]. But you have neglected the more important matters of the law – justice, mercy and faithfulness. You should have practised the latter, without neglecting the former' (v. 23). Jesus was not encouraging them to break the law of tithing. No, he was taking issue with them over their lack of a sense of proportion. God's law contains both ceremonial regulations and moral commandments. But the two, he implied, were not equal; the moral is 'more important' than the ceremonial. Yet it was this that the Pharisees were neglecting in their obsession with ceremonial obligations. So blind were they in this lack of balance, Jesus added with a touch of humour, that they were like people who fuss over a foreign body in their drink. They carefully strain out a tiny gnat and then go and swallow a camel by mistake! (v. 24).

Perhaps the most conspicuous examples of the Jewish leaders' twisted attitudes occurred at the end of Christ's life. Anxious to eat the Passover, they refused to enter the praetorium (where Jesus was on trial before Pilate) 'to avoid ceremonial uncleanness'.[48] Anxious not to contaminate their observance of the Sabbath by permitting the three crucified men to remain on their crosses, they asked Pilate to have their legs broken to speed up their death and the removal of their bodies. They did not see the anomaly of avoiding these comparatively trivial defilements while they were committing the terrible crime of plotting and securing the death of God's Christ.

It is easy to laugh at the Pharisees and to forget that the Pharisaic spirit is by no means dead. But everyone whose view of sin, morality and religion is superficial and external and everyone for whom the ceremonial is more important than the moral is a modern day Pharisee. Some reduce their religion to a few neat and simple rules – for example, a brief prayer or two every day and a church service every Sunday – and imagine that nothing more is required of them.

Others speak and act as if the really important question is whether a Christian refrains from such things as smoking, drinking and wearing make-up. There are some churches in the world which even excommunicate their members for practices like these. But these are the 'mint, dill and cumin' of our day, the herbs of the evangelical's back garden. Although every Christian should come to a careful decision about things like this, it is absurd to equate them with 'the more important matters of the law'.

Still others concentrate on social and cultural taboos like manners, speech or clothing. And if somebody is not dressed in what they regard as the correct way, or does not speak properly, or fails to hold their knife and fork in the proper way and at the correct angle, they are immediately despised and dismissed.

All these are forms of modern Pharisaism. It is as if we come to Jesus and say, 'Lord, why does so-and-so eat with defiled hands?' It is to judge people by purely external criteria, instead of by their moral character. It is to overlook the fact that what defiles people in God's sight is not what is on their outside but on their inside – the evil thoughts of the heart.

4. People matter more than things

Christ's controversy with the Pharisees over morality stressed not only the priority of the inward over the outward and the moral over the ceremonial, but also the personal over the impersonal. He taught that people matter more than things.

It is significant that all but the last two ('arrogance' and 'folly') of the thirteen 'evils' which Jesus listed are social offences, sins against other people. He included breaches of five of the Ten Commandments (murder, adultery, theft, slander and greed) and added malice, deceit and envy. There can be little doubt that he chose his list of 'evils' deliberately. By it he showed that our hearts are not only in revolt against God but also at logger-heads with our neighbour. Furthermore, their concentration on the external and ceremonial showed that the Pharisees neglected love as much as they neglected morality. Their scrupulous concern for ritual niceties was accompanied by a bitter, scornful, critical attitude. So Jesus taught the importance of social right-eousness, and particularly of true caring about people. Twice he quoted God's Word in Hosea 6:6: 'I desire mercy, and not sacrifice.'[49] In other words, according to God's way of seeing things, compassion matters more than ceremonial rules, people matter more than things. Jesus applied this scriptural principle to two practices for which the Pharisees criticized him.

The first was Sabbath-breaking. The disciples were walking through the cornfields one Sabbath day, and, as they did so, were evidently plucking, rubbing and eating the corn. The Pharisees strongly objected to this, no doubt on the grounds that according to their tradition plucking was equivalent to reaping and rubbing to threshing, the point being that activities like this were prohibited on the Sabbath.[50] A little later, in a synagogue, Jesus healed a man with a withered hand.[51] In these two examples, Jesus was, as always, motivated by love. He was concerned that hungry people should be fed and sick people healed. Indeed, he cared enough about their need to break the scribal rules in order to meet it. 'If you had known what these words mean, "I desire mercy, not sacrifice,"' he said to the Pharisees, 'you would not have condemned the innocent.'[52] After all, they themselves took their farm animals to water on the Sabbath,[53] and would go to the rescue of one of their sheep if it fell into a pit on the Sabbath. Did they have more pity for animals than for human beings? As well as this, we note that although they were opposed to Jesus doing good and healing on a Sabbath, they themselves were prepared to do harm and plot to kill him. This is what lies behind his pointed question to them, which Mark records: 'Which is lawful on the Sabbath: to do good or to do evil, to save life or to kill?'[54] In this way he brought their hypocrisy out into the open.

The second issue which led to him repeating the Hosea quotation was the question of spending time with sinners. When Levi-Matthew was converted, he invited his friends and colleagues to a meal to meet Jesus. The Pharisees were appalled to see Jesus in such company. One of the vows they all took on entering the Pharisaic brotherhood was never to be a guest of one of the common people. Yet here was Jesus sitting in a sinner's house and eating with him! Jesus defended his action from the analogy of a doctor and his patients, and then quoted Hosea again: 'Go and learn what this means: "I desire mercy, not sacrifice." For I have not come to call the righteous, but sinners.'[55]

In both cases, the Pharisees were shocked because Jesus had broken their rules. He did it because for him love was the number one virtue. He cared deeply about the hungry, the sick and the sinful, and in order to serve their needs he was prepared to go against the scribal traditions. I do not myself believe that he broke the law of Moses itself. But even if it could be shown conclusively that he did, there is still no justification for taking this as evidence that he set the law aside. The most that could be said is that when two divine laws are in conflict (as sometimes happens in our fallen world), then the law of love takes precedence. This was so in the matter of Corban, for the honour due to parents has priority over the keeping of a rash vow, since people matter more than things. This is the clear implication of his favourite text, 'I desire mercy, and not sacrifice.'

We have seen that the Pharisees' view of morality was superficial because it was external. Any attempt to externalize either
religion or morality today, or to reduce it to a few shallow rules,
is a modern form of Pharisaism. Evangelicals are by no means
always free from this tendency. But it is a hallmark of true
evangelical religion to emphasize that sin and morality are
inward rather than outward, that what defiles us in God's sight
is what comes from the heart, that a new birth is indispensable
to a new life. What pleases God, therefore, is religion and
morality of the heart.

6

Worship: Lips or heart?

Christians believe that true worship is the highest and noblest activity of which human beings, by the grace of God, are capable. It is sad, therefore, that it should ever be a subject of controversy. But it is. If God is seeking worshippers (as Jesus said he was), what kind of worshippers is he looking for? If we are under an obligation to worship God (as the Bible everywhere says we are), what kind of worship should we offer? For not everything that calls itself 'worship' is acceptable to God. On the contrary, while emphasizing our duty to worship God, the Bible also tells us that some worship is actually 'detestable' to him, that he 'hates' and 'despises' it, 'cannot endure' it and therefore rejects it.[1]

Two basic assumptions
This rejection of Israel's worship by God in the seventh and eighth centuries BC was echoed by Jesus in his dealings with the Pharisees of his own day. Indeed, he quoted Isaiah 29:13 as a 'prophecy', by which he meant not simply that this verse

foretold the hypocrisy of the Pharisees, but that it expressed a divinely-revealed principle which was equally applicable to them.

You hypocrites! Isaiah was right when he prophesied about you:

> 'These people honour me with their lips,
>   but their hearts are far from me.
> They worship me in vain;
>   their teachings are merely human rules.'[2]

There are two assumptions here – assumptions shared by Christ and the Pharisees – which those taking part in the modern debates about worship are likely to have in common too.

The first is that worship is a *good* thing. Quoting Isaiah, Jesus said, 'These people *honour me* . . . ' God's problem with the inhabitants of Jerusalem, and Christ's problem with the Pharisees, was not that they honoured God but that they did so in the wrong way. Everyone should honour God by offering to him the honour and glory which he deserves. Indeed, this is the meaning of worship. The very word implies it. For 'worship' is an abbreviation of 'worthship'. It indicates that God is worthy to be praised, that worship is the appropriate recognition of his absolute worth. In worship we come to him – as creatures to honour him as our Creator, as sinners to honour him as our Saviour, as children to honour him as our Father, as servants to honour him as our Lord. Worship is not, therefore, an optional activity which may be added to life's timetable by those who enjoy that sort of thing, and ignored by those who do not. It is an obligation because it is the acknowledgment of plain facts.

The second assumption which underlies the words of Isaiah and of Christ is that worship is something to be done with others in public: '*These people* honour me . . . ' There is of course a place for private worship, the adoration of God by individuals on their own (e.g. 'when you pray, go into your room, close the door and pray to your Father, who is unseen').[3] But the worship referred to here is public, the worship of God by his people when they meet together. Jesus took it for granted that they would assemble for public worship. It is safe to say that he never had in mind a 'religionless Christianity'.

In this further controversy with the Pharisees, then, Jesus is not finding fault with the practice of worship itself, nor with its public and corporate nature. What he is against is its external quality, its formalism, its hypocrisy: 'You *hypocrites*! Isaiah was right when he prophesied about you . . . ' They were not true worshippers at all, but merely actors. The honour they gave to God was all pretence rather than reality. And the essential distinction here is between the worship of the lips and of the heart. Worship is expressed through the lips, but it does not consist of words. Just as the morality acceptable to God is with the heart rather than the hands, so the worship acceptable to God is the humble adoring devotion of the heart rather than what is said to him by the lips. Pharisaic worship is lip-worship; Christian worship is heart-worship.

What, then, are the characteristics of true heart-worship?

Worship based on reason

The first characteristic of heart-worship is that it is based on reason; the mind is fully involved in it. In the Bible the 'heart' is not simply equivalent to the emotions, as it usually is in today's language. In biblical thought the 'heart' is the centre of the human personality and is often used in a way that emphasizes the intellect more than the emotions. Thus, the plea in Proverbs 23:26, 'My son, give me your heart,' has often been understood as an appeal for our love and devotion. But in reality it is a command to listen, to pay attention, to sit up and take notice, an appeal more for concentration than for consecration. This is particularly clear in the book of Proverbs, where we read that the heart should pay attention to 'understanding' and be 'wise'.[4]

Passages in which the 'heart' means above all the 'mind' may be quoted from the New Testament too. Take, for example, the conversion of Lydia, the seller of purple goods who traded in Philippi. Here is how Luke describes her: 'The Lord opened her heart to respond to Paul's message.'[5] In other words, he opened her understanding to grasp and receive the gospel.

Of course the heart includes more than the mind. But it does not include less. So heart-worship is rational worship. To love God with all our heart involves loving him with all our mind.

This leads us to state the first basic principle of Christian worship, which is that we must know God before we can worship him. It is true that Paul found an altar in Athens which was inscribed 'to an unknown God'. But he recognized it as a contradiction in terms. It is impossible to worship an unknown god, since, if he is himself unknown, the kind of worship he desires will be equally unknown. That is why Paul told the philosophers that they were 'ignorant of the very thing you worship – and this is what I am going to proclaim to you'.[6]

The same principle emerges clearly in Christ's conversation with the Samaritan woman at Jacob's well. For more than 700 years the Samaritans and the Jews had developed their religious life independently. This separate development had a political origin, in that the Samaritans were a mixed race descended partly from Israelites and partly from Mesopotamian foreigners who had been settled there in the eighth century BC. But spiritually it was due to their reliance on different Scriptures. The Samaritans accepted the Pentateuch, but rejected the later revelation which God had given of himself through the prophets. Having the law without the prophets, the Samaritans' knowledge of God was incomplete. This is what Jesus referred to in his conversation with the woman by the well: 'You Samaritans worship what you do not know; we [i.e. the Jews] worship what we do know, for salvation [i.e. the promised Messiah] is from the Jews.' Jesus continued: 'Yet a time is coming and has now come when the true worshippers will worship the Father in . . . truth.'[7] So 'true worship' is 'worship in truth'; it is worship of God the Father as he has been fully and finally revealed in Jesus Christ, his Son.

If Samaritan worship was (to say the least) impoverished because of their rejection of the teaching of the prophets, much Jewish worship was spoiled by ritualism. It was lip-worship (the mouthing of meaningless words), not heart-worship (the intelligent adoration of the mind). How could their worship be acceptable to God when they turned a deaf ear to his word spoken through his prophets? Similarly, the Pharisees were rejecting Christ's testimony to the Father; so their worship could not be heart-worship either.

It is because of this fundamental principle that our English Reformers gave us a Book of Common Prayer in the language of the common people, i.e. not in Latin but in English. They also saturated the Prayer Book services in Scripture. All this was deliberate, for the Reformers knew that it is the Word of God which stimulates the worship of God. Worshippers are caught up in the rhythmic swing of the pendulum of hearing and responding to God's Word. So, for example, God speaks through a Scripture sentence and a call to penitence; the congregation respond by confessing their sins. God speaks through the 'absolution' or declaration of his pardon based on biblical promises; the congregation respond in psalms and songs of praise. And so it continues. This principle of rational, biblical worship, which guided Cranmer in composing the Church of England's Prayer Book services, applies equally in every other church, where the worship is 'responsive' to the Word.

And since worship is drawn out and promoted by Scripture, the sermon, too, is essential – at least if it is a true sermon, namely an exposition of the Bible. The same is true of the sacraments. Strictly speaking, the sacraments are not themselves worship, any more than the sermon is worship. For sermon and sacrament are both directed at us rather than God. They proclaim, the one audibly and the other visibly, the glory of God's grace in the salvation of sinners. And so although they are not themselves acts of worship, they *lead to* worship – the adoration of the God who once gave himself for his people and now gives himself to them today.

If the worshippers whom God is seeking are those who draw near to him with their heart and worship him in truth, we must be careful, when we go to church, not to leave our minds behind. We must beware of all forms of worship which appeal to the senses and the emotions but which do not fully engage the mind, especially those which even claim that they are superior forms of worship. No, the only worship that pleases God is heart-worship, and heart-worship is worship based on reason. It is the worship of a rational God who has made us rational beings and given us a rational revelation so that we may worship him rationally, that is to say 'with all our mind'.

This is why the only perfect worship which is offered to God is in heaven, not on earth, because it is only in heaven that God is clearly seen and fully known: 'His servants will serve him, they will see his face, and his name will be on their foreheads.'[8] Because here on earth we 'see only a reflection as in a mirror',[9] even our best worship is bound to be imperfect. But when we see him face to face in heaven, we shall be able to worship him as he is. As the hymn writer John Newton put it:

Weak is the effort of my heart,
And cold my warmest thought,
But when I see Thee as Thou art,
I'll praise Thee as I ought.

Meanwhile, as we remain on earth, our mind must be in our worship. We must listen humbly to the reading and the preaching of God's Word, in order that our knowledge of God may grow. And we must concentrate, giving our whole attention to what we are saying or singing, so that we may worship God for all we have come to know him to be.

Spiritual worship

Heart-worship is spiritual as well as rational. It involves our spirit as well as our mind. We can best explain this by referring again to Christ's conversation with the Samaritan woman. We have already seen that for seven centuries there had been rivalry, often fierce and bitter, between the Jews and the Samaritans. One of the main points of disagreement was the correct place at which to worship. As the woman said to Jesus by the side of the well: 'Our ancestors worshipped on this mountain [i.e. Gerizim], but you Jews claim that the place where we must worship is in Jerusalem.' Jesus responded by telling her that 'a time is coming when you will worship the Father neither on this mountain nor in Jerusalem . . . true worshippers will worship the Father in the Spirit and in truth, for they are the kind of worshippers the Father seeks. God is spirit, and his worshippers must worship in the Spirit and in truth.'[10]

Jesus was saying that the nature of our worship must match up with the nature of the God we are worshipping. If it is the rational worship of a rational God, it is also the spiritual worship of a spiritual God. In contrast to the Samaritans (who rejected three-quarters of the Old Testament), Christian worship is 'in truth'; in contrast to the Pharisees (who focused on external rites), it is 'in spirit'. Because God is spirit, our worship of him is not tied to, or dependent on, any particular place or form. In essence, the worship that pleases God is inward not outward, the praise of the heart not the lips, spiritual not ceremonial. It is not the movement of our bodies in elaborate ritual (however graceful and elegant); it is the movement of our spirit towards him in love and obedience.

This is not to say that there is no need for church buildings. At least in countries where the climate can be unfriendly, they are convenient, not to say essential. But God is not restricted to buildings, still less to particular parts of buildings. Even in Old Testament days, when he allowed for human weakness by causing the brightness of his glory to rest visibly on the mercy seat in the Holy of Holies, spiritually minded Israelites knew that this was merely a symbol of God's presence, and not God himself. As Solomon put it when dedicating his Temple: 'Will God really dwell on earth? The heavens, even the highest heaven, cannot contain you. How much less this temple I have built!'[11]

However, even though God is not tied to buildings, he is bound to his people. To them he has tied himself by the most solemn promise: 'I will be their God, and they shall be my people.'[12] With this covenant went the further promise that he would never 'fail nor forsake' them. And Jesus Christ confirmed this promise of the presence of God with the new Israel: 'For where two or three gather in my name, there am I with them.'[13]

' . . . And surely I am with you always, to the very end of the age.'[14]

If, then, we want to inherit these promises and enjoy the presence of God in our worship, what matters is not the place but the company, not *a* church but *the* church, not a building but God's people. Whenever the people of God have come together, indoors or in the open air, in church or shack, in majestic cathedral or dingy catacomb, these words have come true: 'You have come to Mount Zion, to the city of the living God, the heavenly Jerusalem. You have come to thousands upon thousands of angels in joyful assembly, to the church of the firstborn, whose names are written in heaven. You have come to God, the Judge of all, to the spirits of the righteous made perfect, to Jesus the mediator of a new covenant, and to the sprinkled blood that speaks a better word than the blood of Abel.'[15]

What is true of buildings for worship is equally true of forms of worship. It is not that outward forms are in themselves unnecessary or wrong, any more than are material buildings. To be sure, heart-worship can be silent worship, and we should probably have more periods of silence in our church services. But if it is to involve everyone, it will also be expressed through the lips, that is, in words. These words may be set forms or extempore speech. Both can be the free and sincere utterance of the heart. Both can equally sink to the level of pagan incantation. External forms and ceremonies are harmless, even helpful, but only if they reflect true doctrine and only if they can be appropriate expressions of inward worship.

Let me give a simple example. In some churches the worshippers kneel to pray. It is not necessary to do so. Other Christians sit or stand for prayer. Yet those who kneel like to do so because kneeling seems to express something of the greatness of God and the smallness of human beings in his sight. It also helps them to humble themselves in reverence before him. At the same time, it is perfectly possible to physically bow the knee without ever bowing our heart and will to Christ's commandments.

It is not only possible; it is all too common. No alert reader of the Bible can miss how frequently it warns against the dangers of religious externalism. We have already seen how Christ applied to the Pharisees what Isaiah had spoken several centuries previously to Judah. The worship of the Pharisees was nothing but an outward religious display. The same note of alarm is sounded in many other places. 'You do not delight in sacrifice, or I would bring it; you do not take pleasure in burnt offerings. My sacrifice, O God, is a broken spirit; a broken and contrite heart you, God, will not despise.'[16] The modern church has certainly not grown out of the need for this warning. Colourful ceremonies, rich pageantry and splendid music are neither pleasing to God nor of any benefit to us, unless they are the vehicles of something else, namely spiritual worship.

Evangelical Christians have not always been of one mind about the place of beauty in worship. Some, in their anxiety to heed the warnings of Scripture, have perhaps gone too far in the direction of the austere and the drab, even the sloppy. Others have found that beauty of sight and sound are not necessarily incompatible with inward reality. The same applies to other external accompaniments to worship. Some evangelicals are uninhibited in clapping their hands, swaying their bodies and shouting aloud their Hallelujahs. Others prefer their public worship to be restrained and dignified, remembering that we are to 'worship God acceptably with reverence and awe, for our "God is a consuming fire"'.[17] Since God has made us different people with different temperaments, we should respect one another and give one another freedom in things like this. What all of us must and do insist upon, since the Bible teaches it and Jesus backed it up, is that what concerns God above everything is our heart not our lips, our spirit not our body.

The phrase 'spiritual worship' means more than this, however. It means not only that it is our spirit which worships, but that it is God's Spirit who prompts our worship. 'It is we who are the circumcision,' writes the apostle Paul, emphasizing a vital distinction between Jewish and Christian worship, 'we who serve God by his Spirit . . . '[18] The help of the Spirit is as necessary as the mediation of the Son in our approach to the Father: 'For through him we . . . have access to the Father by one Spirit.'[19] All Christian prayer is through Christ and by the Spirit. The Holy Spirit 'helps us in our weakness'[20] and enables us to cry 'Abba, Father',[21] making us conscious of our relationship to God as his sons and daughters. Besides this, true worship is in a sense contrary to human nature, for human nature is self-centred, while worship is God-centred. Only the Holy Spirit can lift us out of ourselves, turn us inside out and focus our devotion upon God. If worship is stimulated by the Word of God (as we have seen), it is the Spirit of God who uses the Word of God to stimulate it. A prayer to pray often is this one:

> Almighty God, to whom all hearts are open, all desires known, and from whom no secrets are hidden: cleanse the thoughts of our hearts by the inspiration of your Holy Spirit, that we may perfectly love you, and worthily magnify your holy name; through Christ our Lord.

Spiritual worship is inward worship, inspired by the Spirit of God in the spirit of human beings.

Moral worship

Thirdly, true heart-worship is moral as well as rational and spiritual. The conscience is involved, as well as the mind and the spirit.

It is significant that, before Jesus described to the Samaritan woman the kind of worshippers the Father was seeking, he said to her, 'Go, call your husband and come back.' When she replied that she had no husband, Jesus went on: 'You are right when you say you have no husband. The fact is, you have had five husbands, and the man you now have is not your husband. What you have just said is quite true.'[22] Before she could offer the worship Jesus was about to tell her about, her sin must be faced up to, confessed and forgiven.

This is why most forms of public worship are introduced by an act of penitence and confession. This is a clear acknowledgment that we must engage in confession before we are ready to worship. Before we stand for praise, we must kneel in humble penitence. For, 'Who may ascend the mountain of the Lord? Who may stand in his holy place?' The answer is: 'The one who has clean hands and a pure heart . . . '[23] We are not fit to be seen in the courts of heaven in the rags of our sin and guilt.

Again and again the biblical authors insist that worship without morality is positively displeasing to God: 'The Lord detests the sacrifice of the wicked.'[24] 'Does the Lord delight in burnt offerings and sacrifices as much as in obeying the Lord? To obey is better than sacrifice, and to heed is better than the fat of rams.'[25] 'I hate, I despise your religious festivals; your assemblies are a stench to me . . . But let justice roll on like a river, righteousness like a never-failing stream!'[26] 'The multitude of your sacrifices – what are they to me?' says the Lord. 'I have more than enough of burnt offerings, of rams and the fat of fattened animals . . . Stop bringing meaningless offerings! Your incense is detestable to me . . . When you spread out your hands in prayer, I hide my eyes from you; even when you offer many prayers, I am not listening. Your hands are full of blood! Wash and make yourselves clean. Take your evil deeds out of my sight; stop doing wrong. Learn to do right; seek justice. Defend the oppressed. Take up the cause of the fatherless; plead the case of the widow.'[27]

There can be no doubt that this repeated emphasis is necessary. The history of the world has been disfigured by the pursuit of religion without morality, of piety without love. Sometimes the conscience of worshippers has been so blind or hard that they have actually introduced evil into their acts of worship. Perhaps the worst example of this has been the degrading practice of ritual prostitution. But the mingling of devotion to God and injustice to other people is equally perverted. During Israel's religious boom in the eighth century BC, Amos rebuked those who went to the local sanctuaries because he said they 'lie down beside every altar on garments taken in pledge. In the house of their god they drink wine taken as fines [i.e. unjustly so].'[28]

It was the same with the Pharisees in our Lord's day. They attended both synagogue and Temple. They studied the Scriptures. They fasted, prayed and gave to the poor. What they wore, what they said and how they carried themselves all identified them as religious people. Yet their hearts were full of sin, greed and pride. Jesus described them as those who 'devour widows' houses and for a show make long prayers'.[29] In the same way, there are some today who will attend public worship in church, while at the same time negotiating a dishonest business deal, or getting involved in a wrong relationship, or holding onto resentment against someone who has wronged them, or plotting their revenge.

We must reject every claim to genuine religion that is not accompanied by righteousness. The claim to mystical experience without moral obedience is a lie and a delusion. The reason for this, which should be plain, has to do with the very nature of God. 'God is light; in him there is no darkness at all. If we claim to have fellowship with him and yet walk in the darkness, we lie and do not live out the truth . . . Whoever says, "I know him," but does not do what he commands is a liar, and the truth is not in that person . . . Anyone who claims to be in the light but hates a brother or sister is still in the darkness.'[30] The contrast which John repeatedly draws is between what we say and what we are. Religion without righteousness is empty. Faith without works is dead.

The practical point which flows from this unbreakable bond between worship and morality is that worship is much more than a matter of singing hymns or songs and saying prayers. By themselves these things are merely lip-worship. But if they are heart-worship, they are expressing more even than the praise of the mind and of the spirit; they convey in concentrated form the devotion of our whole life. The dedication of the whole week is condensed into an hour or so of public worship on Sunday. Our sacrifice of praise is a token of the sacrifice of ourselves, our souls and our bodies.

Christ's controversy with the Pharisees about worship was that their religion was formal and external. He called it 'hypocrisy' or mere acting. It was worship by the lips alone, and therefore empty, lacking all inward reality. 'They worship me in vain,' he said, quoting Isaiah.

In contrast to Pharisaic worship, Christian worship is heart-worship. However it may be expressed outwardly, it is in essence rational (involving the mind), spiritual (involving both our spirit and God's) and moral (involving the conscience and the whole life). According to Jesus, these are the kind of worshippers the Father is seeking.

7

Responsibility:
Withdrawal or involvement?

What attitude should the followers of Jesus have towards those who do not follow him? There is a wide variety of possibilities, all of which have been adopted by Christian people at different times. Do we despise them, fear them, shun them, tolerate them, condemn them, or seek to serve them? What is the true responsibility of the church to the world around us?

Once again we discover that there was a fundamental difference of attitude in this matter between the Pharisees and Jesus Christ. And once again we have to ask ourselves whether our attitude is Christian (reflecting that of Christ) or Pharisaic (reflecting that adopted by the Pharisees in our Lord's day).

Luke sums up the difference in his editorial introduction to the parables of the lost sheep, lost coin and lost son: 'Now the tax collectors and sinners were all gathering around to hear Jesus. But the Pharisees and the teachers of the law muttered, "This man welcomes sinners and eats with them." '[1]

At first sight the reaction of the Pharisees to the way in which Christ welcomed the tax collectors and sinners may seem surprising, for the Pharisees were keen on winning converts. Jesus himself referred to their enthusiasm for doing so: 'You travel over land and sea to win a single convert.'[2]

But proselytism is not the same as evangelism. To proselytize is to convert somebody else to our opinions and culture, and to squeeze them into our mould; to evangelize is to proclaim God's good news about Jesus Christ so that people will believe in him, find life in him and ultimately be conformed to his image, not ours. The motive behind proselytism is concern for the spread of our own little empire; the motive behind evangelism is concern for the true welfare of other people and ultimately for God's name, kingdom, will and glory.

Now the Pharisees were enthusiastic proselytizers. They loved to draw others into their orbit and subdue them to their influence. But the results, Jesus said, spelled disaster: 'When you have succeeded, you make them twice as much a child of hell as you are.' But if the Pharisees were good at proselytism, they were no good at evangelism, for they had no evangel, no good news and no compassion either. So, when the tax collectors and sinners were all flocking to Jesus, they complained instead of rejoicing.

It is important to understand what lay behind the radically different attitude to sinners adopted by Christ and by the Pharisees.

The attitude of the Pharisees

The seed from which Pharisaism sprang was good seed. It was the Old Testament doctrine of the church as the holy people of God.

Like all good Jews, the Pharisees knew the history of what made the nation of Israel special. God had chosen Abraham and his descendants, and had promised to be their God. He confirmed his covenantal promise to Isaac and to Jacob and to Jacob's descendants, the so-called 'children of Israel'. He renewed his covenant with them at Mount Sinai after delivering them from slavery in Egypt. 'I will take you as my own people,' he said, 'and I will be your God.'[3] He expresses it more fully a little later: 'If you obey me fully and keep my covenant, then out of all nations you will be my treasured possession. Although the whole earth is mine, you will be for me a kingdom of priests and a holy nation.'[4]

But Israel disobeyed God's voice and broke his covenant 'until the wrath of the Lord was aroused against his people and there was no remedy',[5] with the result that the second – the Babylonian – captivity began. Then, yet again, God remembered and renewed his covenant with his chosen people, redeemed them from their exile and brought them back to the Promised Land. And when they returned, they were determined as never before to be a separate people, holy unto the Lord their God. They 'separated themselves from the neighbouring peoples for the sake of the Law of God'.[6] They decided not to intermarry with them, nor to break the Sabbath through trading with them.

The repatriated exiles went further than this, however. Because they misunderstood the nature of the holiness God required of them, they began to cultivate a false separatism. They forgot the prophetic description of their destiny to be 'a light to the nations'.[7] Instead, they withdrew from all contact with the nations around them. And so Pharisaism was born. The real parting of the ways arrived when Palestine became absorbed into the far-flung empire of Alexander the Great, and Greek influence started to infiltrate into Judaism. Some Jews surrendered to it (the Hellenists) while others resisted it (the Hasidaeans, from *Hasidim* or 'pious ones'). The Sadducees came out of the Hellenists and the Pharisees emerged from the Hasidaeans.

The very word 'Pharisees' is an accurate description of them, for it is in fact an Aramaic term for 'separatists'. The Pharisees were the religious exclusives of their day. In their determination to conform strictly to the law, they kept their distance from any and every contact that (in their view) might 'defile' them. This meant avoiding, not only non Jews or Gentiles, together with Hellenized Jews, but also the 'common people'. Because of their ignorance of the law, the common people no doubt broke it and so, as law-breakers, were unclean.

The superior and scornful attitude which the Pharisees adopted towards the ordinary people appears several times in the Gospels. When they were disturbed by the early popularity of Jesus, they put it down to the people's ignorance. They asked sarcastically, 'Have any of the rulers or of the Pharisees believed in him? No! But this mob that knows nothing of the law – there is a curse on them.'[8] So well known was this Pharisaic contempt for the common herd that Jesus used it to explain what the local church's excommunication of a sinner who refused to repent would mean. We should treat him like 'a pagan and a tax collector',[9] he said, that is, as the Pharisees treat such people. Indeed, the very phrase 'tax collectors and sinners' was borrowed from the vocabulary of the Pharisees. 'Sinners' was their scornful description not for a particularly disreputable section of the community but for all the common people who failed to observe the traditions of the elders, the ceremonial rules which the Pharisees and their predecessors had laid down. 'Tax collectors' were added as a specific example of what it was to be a 'sinner'. Because they were employed by the pagans, they were inevitably defiled. The Pharisees viewed 'tax collectors and sinners' as beyond the pale, the outcasts of spiritual society. Imagine their horror when Jesus ate and drank with them, and actually welcomed them into his company![10]

The Pharisees would never have dreamed of associating with 'sinners' themselves. Indeed, they took active steps to avoid the very possibility. They banded themselves together in a closed brotherhood. Calling themselves the *Haberim*, the 'associates', they pledged themselves to obey all the regulations of the ceremonial law and the traditions of the elders. In particular, as we saw in an earlier chapter, they undertook by a solemn vow to tithe everything they ate, bought and sold, and not to be guests of the common people, nor to entertain them as guests in their own clothes, nor to trade any food with them.

So the Pharisaic doctrine of holiness, of separation from the world, was a warped doctrine. Instead of seeking to be truly holy in thought, word and deed by demonstrating love and care to those around them, they withdrew from social contact with 'sinners' and despised those who did not follow their example. They became a 'holy club', a religious closed shop which had as little to do with the world around as possible. They also became harsh and critical; they had no compassion for people in ignorance, sin or need.

The attitude of Jesus

That 'tax collectors and sinners were all gathering around to hear Jesus'[11] shows immediately that Jesus' attitude to them was totally different from that of the Pharisees. Indeed, the Pharisees were scandalized by his free and easy contact with people with whom they would never spend time. Even his own disciples took a while to get used to his generous and open attitude.

The Gospel writers give us numerous illustrations of the difference between the Pharisaic and the Christian attitudes to people in need. They emphasize that Jesus Christ showed compassion for everyone, no matter how much they were despised and rejected by others.

For example, when some parents tried to bring their children to Jesus, wanting him to bless them, the disciples 'rebuked' them. They supposed that Jesus would take no interest in children, for children were 'not . . . loved in antiquity as now they are; no halo of romance and tenderness encircled them; too often they were subjected to shameful cruelties and hard neglect'.[12] But 'When Jesus saw this, he was indignant. He said to them, "Let the little children come to me, and do not hinder them, for the kingdom of God belongs to such as these . . ." And he took the children in his arms, placed his hands on them and blessed them.'[13]

It was much the same with a blind beggar called Bartimaeus, who was sitting by the roadside outside the gates of Jericho. When he heard that Jesus was passing by, he began to shout, 'Jesus, Son of David, have mercy on me!' But many people in the crowd (including some of the disciples perhaps?) 'rebuked him'. They told him to be quiet, implying that Jesus had no time for the likes of him. But he refused to be silenced and shouted all the more, 'Son of David, have mercy on me!' We read that Jesus stopped, ordered him to be brought to him, asked him what he wanted and restored to him his sight.[14]

One of six things that rabbis were not permitted to do was to talk with a woman in public, even (according to one rabbi) with his own wife! This is why, when he spoke freely with a woman of Samaria at Jacob's well and his disciples returned from the village and found them together, 'they were surprised to find him talking with a woman'.[15]

The Pharisees would gather up their robes and draw back in self-righteous horror if a prostitute came near them. But Jesus allowed one not only to approach him, but to bathe his feet with her tears, wipe them with her hair, kiss them and anoint them with ointment. Simon the Pharisee, his host on that occasion, was appalled.[16]

In those days it was said that 'Jews do not associate with Samaritans'.[17] But Jesus was an exception to the rule and refused to be bound by this tradition. The conversation he had at Jacob's well was with a person who was despised three times over – as a Samaritan, a woman and a sinner. But Jesus did not despise her.

The law of Moses contained some careful regulations about leprosy, no doubt for hygienic reasons. The rabbis went far beyond these precautionary measures. Thinking that those who suffered with leprosy were under God's judgment, they loathed them and even threw stones at them to drive them away. In contrast to this cruelty, Jesus had compassion on them. When one came to him, kneeling before him and begging him for help, Jesus did something unheard of. He actually 'reached out his hand and touched him'[18] and healed him.

In the same way, he touched those who were sick. When many people suffering from various diseases were brought to him, we read that 'laying his hands on each one, he healed them'.[19] Especially striking was his concern for the woman who 'had been subject to bleeding for twelve years'. The contemporary Jewish view of her condition went well beyond the Mosaic rules of hygiene. But when she came behind Jesus in the crowd and touched his clothes, though he asked her to declare herself, he did not tell her off for what she had done. Instead, he spoke words of tenderness to her and sent her away in health and peace.[20] He did not stop at physical contact with the sick; he even took the hand of a girl who was dead – something no Pharisee would ever have dreamed of doing – and restored her to life.[21]

Finally, in this list of people the Pharisees despised and shunned, we come back to 'tax collectors and sinners'. The Pharisee's prayer in the parable was typical of their attitude: 'God, I thank you that I am not like other people – robbers, evildoers, adulterers – or even like this tax collector.'[22] In their view, the tax collectors were classed alongside the dishonest and the immoral. They would not think of accepting an invitation to visit the home of such disreputable people. Jesus, on the other hand, invited himself into the home of Zacchaeus, the notorious tax collector of Jericho, which provoked the reaction, 'He has gone in to be the guest of a sinner'[23] (in breach of one of the Pharisees' basic vows). When another tax collector named Levi-Matthew responded to the call of Christ, he hosted 'a great banquet for Jesus at his house' to celebrate his conversion; 'and a large crowd of tax collectors and others were eating with them'. Once again, and predictably enough, the Pharisees and teachers of the law complained: 'Why do you eat and drink with tax collectors and sinners?'[24] But Jesus went further than attending a party in Levi-Matthew's home – he was audacious enough to include him in his team of apostles. He did not regard him as in any way unclean or hold back from this close association with him.

In all these Gospel incidents, we see the distance that separated Jesus from the Pharisees. The Pharisees withdrew from contact with all outcasts. Jesus, however, welcomed them as friends; he touched untouchables.

Why was this? What was the cause of this disagreement between them? The answer is simple: the Pharisees' chief concern was *themselves* and how to preserve their own purity, whereas Jesus Christ's top priority was other people – how 'to seek and to save the lost'.[25]

In order to explain and defend what he did, Jesus resorted to a number of telling pictures or parables.

To begin with, he likened himself to a doctor who spends himself in his care for the sick and risks catching their infection in order to do so. This is how he answered the Pharisees' indignant question about why he ate with tax collectors and sinners. 'It is not the healthy who need a doctor,' he said, 'but those who are ill. I have not come to call the righteous, but sinners.'[26]

Again, when the Pharisees grumbled, saying, 'This man welcomes sinners and eats with them,'[27] he replied by likening himself to a shepherd who had lost one of his hundred sheep. He would not abandon the missing one, nor wait hopefully for it to bleat its way home. He would rather abandon the ninety-nine that were safe in order to go out after the one that was lost and in danger. He would go on searching until he found it. And the discovery would lead to rejoicing, in which he would want his friends and neighbours to share.[28] What distinguished Jesus from the Pharisees was, in a word, 'grace', the divine initiative which first seeks and then saves the lost sinner. As the Jewish scholar C. G. Montefiore explained, 'The Rabbis had said that if the sinner returns to God, God will receive him: they had not said that the love of God goes out to seek the sinner where he is. But in the Gospels it is so.'[29]

We move from a shepherd who lost one of his hundred sheep to a woman who lost one of her ten coins. Perhaps the drachma, the silver coin she had mislaid, had sentimental as well as monetary value. It may have been an ornament, or one of the ten silver coins which Palestinian women wore in those days to show they were married, rather like the modern wedding ring. At all events, when she lost it, she missed it. It did not occur to her just to accept her loss. Instead, she lit a lamp and swept the whole house, conducting a thorough search for it until she found it. And again, with the recovered coin as with the recovered sheep, the discovery led to rejoicing and the rejoicing to a celebration which friends and neighbours were invited to join. Even so, Jesus said, there is 'rejoicing in heaven', 'rejoicing in the presence of the angels of God' over just one, single, sinner who repents. It was this that the Pharisees lacked. They did not rejoice; they grumbled.[30]

The longest of the three parables about lostness (the Prodigal Son) illustrates the same basic truth about divine compassion, but goes deeper and adds the further theme of the elder brother. The grace of God in the ministry of Christ, already exhibited in the doctor, the shepherd and the woman, is now seen in the father. And it is not difficult to see the parallels between, first, the tax collectors and the prodigal son and secondly, the Pharisees and the elder brother.[31]

We should not minimize the rebelliousness of the younger son. When he later confessed, 'I have sinned', he was telling the truth. He had lost both his fortune through foolishness and his honour through sin. He could hardly have sunk any lower. Not only had he lost everything he possessed; he was himself lost.

But all the time his father remained on the look-out for him and never gave up hope. His patience did not waver. His love did not fade. He persevered. And when at last he caught sight of the returning boy, while he was still some distance away, immediately he 'was filled with compassion for him; he ran to his son, threw his arms around him and kissed him'.[32]

Once more the emphasis is on the initiative of grace. The father did not wait for his son to reach home; he ran out to meet and welcome him. He did not wait for him to make amends. He did not relegate him to the life of service he knew he deserved. No, he instantly reinstated him as a son in the family and honoured him with a ring, with sandals and with the best robe. He did not even wait until the boy had finished his apology; he interrupted him to order a feast.

But as everyone began to celebrate, a shadow was cast on the party by the gloomy refusal of the elder brother to join in. Learning what had given rise to the music and dancing, he became angry and refused to go in, despite the appeals made to him by his father. He resented the welcome accorded to his brother, especially as his own loyalty to the father didn't seem to him to have been adequately recognized. He represents those who see religion as being about what people deserve, those to whom the idea of grace is unjust, even immoral. He knew nothing of the guilt which no human merit can wash away, nothing of the divine offer of an undeserved forgiveness, nothing of heavenly joy over sinners who repent. He was harsh, sour, self-righteous and callous. While others celebrated, he stayed away and sulked. In brief, he was a Pharisee.

The Pharisees saw Christ's acceptance of outcasts as an inexcusable compromise with sin; they did not see it for what it really was, an expression of the divine compassion towards sinners.

The attitude of the Christian church

Leaving the first century and entering our own, we need to ask what the attitude of today's church is towards outsiders. Is it Pharisaic, or is it Christian? I fear that it is often Pharisaic. That is, the church tends (just as it has always done) to withdraw from the world and leave it to its own devices. Evangelicals have by no means been free of this tendency, even though it goes completely against what we say we believe. Let me try to expand on what I think are the four commonest ways in which we see this.

1. *Self-righteousness*. It is the attitude of the elder brother who thinks that the sinner should be left to stew in his own juice – even though he may not actually say it like this. 'Sinners get

what they deserve; it simply serves them right.' We do not use
language like this, but this is the image which we often present
to the world. To the outsider the church is often not inviting
but forbidding, smugly satisfied with itself and harshly condemning of others. Non-Christians sometimes say that they
find more acceptance, more compassionate understanding of
human shortcomings in the world than in the church. To them
the church lacks warmth and is even positively inhuman.

In saying this, I do not want the church either to ignore sin
or to do away with the need for repentance, but only to offer
people what Bishop David Sheppard used to call an 'unjudging
friendship'. Otherwise, we give the impression that the church
is for saints, not sinners. Yes, it is composed of 'saints' in the
New Testament sense that every Christian belongs to God and
to the 'holy' ('separate') people of God. But saints are also still
sinners. Human nature remains fallen and we often fail. We are
far from perfect and it is only by God's sheer grace that we
are becoming in character and conduct what we already are in
our standing before him.

The 'holiness' of the church is more about what it is called
to be as the people of God than what it actually is at present.
Pharisaism is a false claim to holiness, a false view of the church.
It turns the church into a preserve for the impeccably respect-
able, a museum of rare spiritual exhibits, instead of a convalescent
home for the sin-sick, a refuge for the helpless and a hostel
for travellers.

What would happen in the average local church if an
outspoken militant atheist or a well-known prostitute were
converted? Would they be welcomed? As Georges Michonneau
once put it: 'Oh, we accept Mary Magdalene because she is in
the Gospel, but I should like to see her walk into one of our
meetings! We read about the reluctance with which the Christian

Jews of Jerusalem received Saul the persecutor, when he appeared before them as a new convert – and we find their attitude astonishing; I should like to see him drop into one of our men's groups!'[33]

Another aspect of this false view of the church is the way Pharisaism can sometimes appear in racial and social attitudes. Whenever the church is more exclusive in its membership than Scripture indicates, it has become Pharisaic. What unites the church is a common faith in Christ and a common share in the Spirit. Apart from this one essential, Christians need have nothing else in common at all. We differ from one another in temperament, personality, education, colour, culture, citizenship, language and in many other ways. Thank God we do. The church is a wonderfully inclusive fellowship, in which there is 'neither Jew nor Gentile, neither slave nor free, nor is there male and female'.[34] In other words, in Christ we have equality. Distinctions of race and status, which are causes of division in other communities, have no place in the Christian community. To bring such things into Christian fellowship is to destroy it. 'Birds of a feather flock together' may be true in nature, but it is not a Christian proverb. The glory of the church is not our likeness to one another, but our *un*likeness. Therefore to reject a believer because of something different about them is to abandon Christ and join the Pharisees.

2. The church withdraws from the world because of a genuine if mistaken *fear of contamination*. This is the spirit of monasticism. We should not condemn it completely, for it is the distortion of a fine ideal. It begins with a true biblical recognition that 'the world', human society which turns its back on the rule of God, or simply godless secularism, is evil. It goes on to hear, and to desire to obey, the biblical commands not to love the world, nor to be shaped by it, but rather to keep oneself

from being polluted by the world.[35] But then it takes a wrong turning. It assumes that the only effective way to avoid conforming to worldly standards is to avoid the company of worldly people, that the way to renounce worldliness is to leave the world. The desire is right but the deduction is a serious mistake.

In saying this we are not questioning the sincerity of all monks and nuns. Nor are we denying the debt owed by the Christian world to the religious orders. Though some were far from what they should have been, others have been notable islands of Christian culture in a turbulent sea of paganism.

Nevertheless, we must insist that this is not a truly Christian ideal. Because it is a withdrawal from the world, it is an expression of Pharisaism, whose danger Jesus seems to have envisaged when he uttered his petition: 'My prayer is not that you take them out of the world but that you protect them from the evil one.'[36]

It needs to be added that many contemporary Christians who have never seen the inside of a monastery or convent are nonetheless 'monastic' in outlook. That is, they live a life of religious seclusion, insulated from the world. They have little if any concern for others outside their own fellowship, being concerned rather with the business of self-preservation. It is this distortion which leads, more than anything else, to 'religionless Christianity'. Given the emptiness of much of what passes for 'religion', it would be better for Christianity to be 'religionless'! We need to say that 'religion' in the sense of public worship is an important aspect of Christianity. But such worship is unacceptable if it exists on its own and if those taking part have no comparable concern to live in the world as both witnesses and servants. A church which lives for itself alone must die. It is Pharisaic, not Christian. A truly Christian church exists for God and for others.

3. A third modern form of Pharisaism has to do with the relation between *evangelism and social concern*. What is God's purpose (and therefore the church's responsibility) for the world?

One point of view is that God's chief concern is the salvation of individual souls and that the church's only responsibility is to proclaim the gospel. This means that the call to get involved in any kind of social action must be firmly resisted. I think this exclusive emphasis on personal salvation is a good deal less common among evangelicals than some people think. Nevertheless, it is a tendency to be aware of.

At the other end of the scale is the view that God's chief concern is not with the church but with the world. And what he wants to bring about in the world, we are told, is shalom, 'peace', the harmony within community which God intends society to enjoy. According to this kind of thinking, shalom is almost equivalent to the kingdom of God, and the church's mission is to discover what God is doing in the world and catch up with it.

Such a quest for better social structures has sometimes replaced the quest for individual conversions, while the proclamation of the gospel is replaced by the kind of dialogue in which the Christian meets the non-Christian on equal terms so that they can pool their ideas.

These approaches to evangelism and social concern, although at opposite extremes, are actually quite like each other in that both contain an element of Pharisaism. For each side's involvement with the world is limited, unbalanced, and less than fully Christian.

The kind of evangelicalism which concentrates exclusively on saving individual souls is not true evangelicalism. It fails to be evangelical because it fails to be biblical. It forgets that God did not create just souls but body-souls called human beings, who are also social beings, and that he cares about their bodies and their society as well as about their relationship with himself and their eternal destiny. This is why true Christian love will care for people as people, and will seek to serve them, neglecting neither the soul for the body nor the body for the soul. Indeed, the fact is that evangelicals have often been at the forefront of social and political action.

We saw earlier how brightly Christ's compassion for outcasts shone against the dark background of the Pharisees' indifference. There are still groups in our society that tend to be neglected – for example, drug addicts, alcoholics, the mentally ill and the elderly – who need what might be termed 'total care'. They challenge us to bold action, which combines gospel truth *and* practical service in a balanced expression of love.

Those who concentrate exclusively on questions of social justice, however, forget the Christian 'saying that deserves full acceptance: Christ Jesus came into the world to save sinners',[37] and forget also the plain commission to the church to proclaim repentance and forgiveness to all nations.[38]

As Dr W. A. Visser 't Hooft, a former General Secretary of the World Council of Churches, once put it, 'A Christianity which has lost its vertical dimension has lost its salt and is not only insipid in itself; but useless for the world. But a Christianity which would use the vertical preoccupation as a means to escape from its responsibility for and in the common life of man is a denial of the Incarnation, of God's love for the world manifested in Christ.'[39]

4. In our efforts to find examples in the contemporary church of Pharisaic withdrawal from the world, we have so far discussed self-righteousness, a monastic type of self-absorbed isolationism and an unbalanced emphasis on evangelism or social concern, each at the expense of the other. But the fourth and perhaps the

commonest reason why we tend to stand apart from the world is plain *laziness and selfishness*. We do not want to get involved in its hurt or dirt. Only the compassion of Christ will overcome our reluctance.

Self-righteousness and snobbery, fear of contamination, a distorted view of the relationship between soul and body, and apathy. Underlying these four causes of withdrawal there lurks a false view of God. The God revealed by Jesus Christ is a God who cares. He loves people who do not deserve to be loved. He causes his sun to rise on the evil as well as the good, and sends rain on the unrighteous as well as the righteous. He made us body-souls and cares for us as body-souls. And he has taken action – sacrificial action – to supply an antidote for our sin. He has got himself deeply involved in our predicament.

Jesus Christ did not remain aloof, or refuse to get involved, or hide away in the safe immunity of heaven. He entered our world. He assumed our nature. He identified himself with our humanity. He allowed himself to experience our temptations, sorrows and pains. He made friends with outcasts and received the nickname 'friend of tax collectors and sinners'.[40] He humbled himself to serve people in their need. He washed his disciples' feet. He never drew back from any demanding situation. He was willing finally to bear our sins and our curse in our place.

And now he says to the church: 'As the Father has sent me, I am sending you.'[41] The church's mission reflects the Son's mission, and both express the character of the Father. What is this? He is not the Judge only, but the Saviour. He does not reward merit, but he does bestow mercy. He is the shepherd of lost sheep, the doctor of sick souls, a father of infinite patience. Now he sends us out into the world just like he sent Christ – not to run away and escape, but to enter the pain of distressed humanity, to think and feel our way into people's doubts, difficulties and distresses, to be channels of the love of God as both servants and witnesses, to bring what relief we can and the good news of salvation through Christ's death and resurrection. This is our responsibility. Nothing less than costly involvement is Christian; to withdraw is Pharisaic. 'As our Lord took on our flesh, so he calls his Church to take on the secular world.' To refuse to do so is to refuse to 'take the Incarnation seriously'.[42]

The conclusion brings us to one of the great paradoxes of Christian living. The whole church (and every member of it) is called as much to involvement in the world as to separation from it, as much to 'worldliness' as to 'holiness'. Not to a worldliness which is unholy, nor to a holiness which is unworldly, but to 'holy worldliness', a true separation to God which is lived out in the world – the world which he made and sent his Son to redeem.

Only the power of God can deliver us from the grudging, judging attitude of the elder brother, from the false Pharisaic fear of contamination-by-contact and from the detachment which refuses to get involved. In place of all this we need the compassion of Christ. The Pharisees of today's church can grumble if they want to – as long as they also say of us (as their ancient counterparts said of our Master): 'This man welcomes sinners and eats with them.'

8

Ambition:
Our glory or God's?

Hidden motives play a large part in how we behave. The important question to ask is not merely what a person is doing, but
why they are doing it. Psychology is concerned to probe our
basic motivation. Industry and commerce study the subject
of incentives in order first to attract good staff and then to
encourage good work.

Certainly none of us can know ourselves until we have
honestly asked ourselves about our motives. What is the driving-
force of my life? What ambition dominates and directs me?

Ultimately, there are only two controlling ambitions, to
which all others come down in the end. One is our own glory,
and the other God's. In John's Gospel we find them set them in
irreconcilable opposition to each other as we discover Christ's
fundamental quarrel with the Pharisees: 'They loved human
praise more than praise from God.'[1]

Glory to God not to others
To love the glory of God more than the glory of other people
is to seek to bring glory to him rather than to others. It is to

desire that everyone will honour God (rather than us or others), and that we and they will give him the glory that he deserves. It is to fulfil the desires expressed in the Lord's Prayer, to be concerned for the hallowing of God's name, the coming of God's kingdom and the doing of God's will.

Jesus Christ was filled with this desire. 'I am not seeking glory for myself,'[2] he could say. Again, 'Whoever speaks on their own does so to gain personal glory, but he who seeks the glory of the one who sent him is a man of truth; there is nothing false about him.'[3]

'Father,' he prayed, 'glorify your name!'[4] This was the dominating passion of his life and ministry, so that he could claim at the end, 'I have brought you glory on earth by finishing the work you gave me to do.'[5]

In this same ambition lay what was perhaps the greatest single secret of the strength of the Protestant Reformation. One of the essential differences between pre-Reformation religion and Reformation religion is that the former was in many respects human-centred, while the Reformers were determined to be God-centred. In the matter of authority they rejected human traditions, because they believed in the supremacy and the sufficiency of God's Word written. In the matter of salvation they rejected the merits of human beings, because they believed in the complete effectiveness of Christ's finished work. This is why they emphasized the doctrine of justification by grace alone through faith alone. This, too, is why they rejected the Mass. They were utterly appalled by the idea that the Mass was in any sense a sacrifice because they saw it as insulting to the glory of Christ's only and perfect sacrifice. Cranmer went so far as to call it 'the greatest blasphemy and injury that can be done against Christ'.[6] The Reformers' reasons for all this protest were plain. In emphasizing that the church's authority came from the

Bible alone (*sola scriptura*) and that the sinner's salvation was by *grace alone* (*sola gratia*) through *faith alone* (*sola fides*), their motive in both was *to the glory of God alone* (*soli Deo Gloria*).

The Reformers turned their backs on Pharisaism. For the Pharisees were obsessed with the quest for glory. They were not concerned to bring glory to God; they wanted it for themselves. We shall see later how this impaired the whole of their lives. At this point we need just to pause and see how much Pharisaism remains even in Christian hearts. Indeed, our nature is such that, even in our most sacred moments, we may find ourselves motivated by concern for our glory rather than God's. Examples may be found in our worship, our evangelism and our ministry.

True heart-worship is the most God-centred, God-honouring activity in which we either can or will ever participate. It is to credit God with the glory due to his name, to be occupied with God and with God alone. Nothing so disinfects us of self-centredness.

Yet how subtly and swiftly can selfish vanity intrude into public worship! The minister becomes proud of the way he is leading the service, the preacher of his eloquence and learning, the choir and organist of their musical ability and the congregation of their piety in being in church at all! Just when our attention should be absorbed exclusively with God in self-forgetful adoration, we become self-conscious, self-righteous, self-important and self-congratulatory again.

True evangelism is closely allied to true worship. Paul calls it a sacrificial service in which evangelists become priests as they offer their converts to God. Evangelism is also a proclamation of the gospel by which people are rescued from self-centredness and liberated into God-centredness. Yet much of our evangelism is human-centred. Our publicity draws attention to the speaker or the sponsor more than the Saviour. We become proud of our organization or puffed up with conceit over our own evangelistic enthusiasm.

Or take, as a third example, the exercise of ministry in the church. 'Ministry' means 'service' – lowly, menial service; it is, therefore, curiously perverse to turn it into an occasion for boasting. Jesus specifically distinguished between 'rule' and 'service', 'authority' and 'ministry', and added that, though the former was characteristic of pagans, the latter was to characterize his followers: 'You know that those who are regarded as rulers of the Gentiles lord it over them, and their high officials exercise authority over them. Not so with you. Instead, whoever wants to become great among you must be your servant, and whoever wants to be first must be slave of all. For even the Son of Man did not come to be served, but to serve, and to give his life as a ransom for many.'[7] Thus Christian ministers are to take as their model the Christ who came to serve, not the Gentiles (or the Pharisees) who preferred to be lords.

This is not to deny that some authority attaches to the ministry, but rather to define and limit it.[8] It is the authority which stems from sound teaching and consistent example. It is never authoritarian to the extent that someone attempts to dominate another's mind, conscience or will. 'Not lording it over those entrusted to you, but being examples to the flock.'[9] Yet lording it is exactly what the Pharisees were doing, keeping the people in subjection under them.

Jesus exposed the tyranny of the Pharisees by drawing attention to the revealing titles which they loved. He insisted that in the church he was founding such titles were not to be used: 'But you are not to be called "Rabbi", for you have one Teacher, and you are all brothers. And do not call anyone on earth "father", for you have one Father, and he is in heaven. Nor are you to be called instructors, for you have one Instructor, the Messiah.'[10] In other words, no-one is to be involved in a child–father relationship of dependence or a servant–master relationship of unquestioning obedience or a pupil–teacher relationship of uncritical acceptance. Each of these attitudes is doubly wrong. For one thing it disrupts Christian fellowship: 'You are all brothers.' For another it assumes rights which belong to God alone: 'You have one Father (on whom you depend), and he is in heaven', 'you have one Instructor (whom you are to obey), the Messiah and (Jesus might have added) you have one Guide (whose instruction you are to follow), the Holy Spirit'. Domination by clergy or ministers is an offence both to God and humanity, to the three Persons of the Trinity and to the fellowship of believers.

The apostle Paul had learned this lesson well. He was horrified when the Corinthian church split into factions, declaring their allegiance to Paul, Apollos and Cephas (i.e. Peter).[11] It may be that the further slogan 'I belong to Christ' was not so much the cry of a fourth party as the apostle's own response. That is, if the Corinthians will insist on giving their loyalty to human beings, let it at least be clear that Paul belonged to Christ. Actually, of course, they did as well, even though their behaviour contradicted it. They had believed and been baptized into the name of Christ, not Paul. It wasn't that they belonged to Paul but that Paul and his fellow-apostles belonged to them: 'All things are yours, whether Paul or Apollos or Cephas or the world or life or death or the present or the future – all are yours, and you are of Christ, and Christ is of God.'[12]

If only the church of later generations had remembered and obeyed its Lord's command as clearly as the apostle Paul! It is true that most of the Christian leaders raised up by God have been as concerned as he was when people focus on them rather than on their Lord. Martin Luther's plea is one to reflect on:

'Please do not use my name; do not call yourselves Lutherans, but Christians.'[13] But their followers have not always been so sensible or modest. John Venn, Rector of Clapham at the beginning of the nineteenth century, pulled no punches on this issue:

> It was a wise precept delivered by our blessed Lord to call no man master. Would to God that the names of Calvin and Arminius, as leaders of a party, had, like the body of Moses, been buried in oblivion. It should be the peculiar glory of the Church of Christ that it has but one master, the best, the wisest and the highest. By ranging under the banners of a party, we in effect desert those of Christ, and imbibe a spirit which is far more opposite to Christianity than any deviation in non-essential points from the Christian faith. Love to the brethren was laid down by our great Master, as the characteristic of his disciples, but, wherever a party spirit is embraced, there the love, which like that of Christ should be universal, is narrowed and confined to a set; and Christian character degenerates into a mode of selfishness.[14]

As we look back over these different examples of vanity, we have seen that our worship, our evangelism and our ministry all become contaminated whenever the focus shifts from bringing glory to God to bringing glory to ourselves or other people.

Approval from God rather than others

To love the glory of God more than our own glory is also to seek approval from God rather than other people.

This too was what Jesus declared to be his ambition. 'I do not accept glory from human beings,'[15] he said. Indeed, we know that he was despised and rejected, even by his own people, and died as an outcast on a Roman cross. Yet God approved him. Both at his baptism and at the transfiguration God affirmed

Jesus as his Son, whom he loved and with whom he was well pleased, and then finally vindicated him by the resurrection and the ascension.

The ambition of the Pharisees, however, was very different. Their chief concern was to be highly regarded by other people, rather than God, and this made a negative impact on every aspect of their lives.

First, it prevented their conversion. The reason why they did not believe in Jesus was their fear of public opinion. 'How can you believe,' Jesus asked, 'since you accept glory from one another but do not seek the glory that comes from the only God?'[16] As Jesus made himself known to them as Messiah, Son of God and Saviour, their chief concern was 'What will the Sanhedrin think?' Their vanity blinded them to Christ's glory. It is the same today. 'Fear of man will prove to be a snare.'[17] Jesus Christ still says to those who would follow him, 'If anyone is ashamed of me and my words in this adulterous and sinful generation, the Son of Man will be ashamed of them when he comes in his Father's glory with the holy angels.'[18]

Secondly, it silenced their witness. It explains two things: first, why most did not believe in him and secondly, why the few who did believe in him remained secret disciples and did not acknowledge him openly. John writes that towards the end of his ministry 'many even among the leaders believed in him. But because of the Pharisees they would not openly acknowledge their faith for fear they would be put out of the synagogue; for they loved human praise more than praise from God.'[19] Their eyes were on other people. They could not bear the prospect of the ridicule and rejection which would follow an open commitment to Christ. They were hungry for popularity and praise. The same self-regarding anxiety to stand high in the opinion of others keeps many Christians dumb today when they should speak up for their Lord. It also ruins the ministry of every preacher who is more concerned to please the congregation than the Master (theirs and his). 'Not only when their eye is on you and to curry their favour, but with sincerity of heart and reverence for the Lord'[20] is an instruction just as applicable to ministers of the gospel as it is to employees. Our ministry will never be blessed by God until we can join Paul in declaring, 'Am I now trying to win the approval of human beings, or of God? Or am I trying to please people? If I were still trying to please people, I would not be a servant of Christ.'[21]

Thirdly, it spoiled their social behaviour. Their quest for their own glory contaminated the way they behaved in public. This is how Jesus summed up the teachers of the law and the Pharisees: 'Everything they do is done for people to see: They make their phylacteries wide and the tassels on their garments long; they love the place of honour at banquets and the most important seats in the synagogues; they love to be greeted with respect in the market-places and to be called "Rabbi" by others.'[22] In the clothes they wore, in the functions they attended, in the seats they occupied, and in the deferential greetings and titles they were given, they enjoyed being conspicuous and receiving honour from other people. Indeed, they went out of their way to win admiration from others.

Fourthly, and most seriously of all, it ruined their religious practice, their 'piety'. In the Sermon on the Mount Jesus warned his disciples against following their bad example. 'Be careful not to practise your righteousness in front of others to be seen by them,' he said (Matthew 6:1). Jesus then went on to give three particular examples – giving (vv. 2–4), praying (vv. 5, 6) and fasting (vv. 16–18). These three practices were much emphasized by the Pharisees, all of whom gave money to the poor, spent time in prayer and abstained from food for spiritual purposes.

Jesus had no problem with the three practices themselves. On the contrary, since he began each paragraph with the words 'when you . . . ' (not 'if you . . . '), he clearly expected his disciples to do the same things. They express, at least in part, our three-fold Christian duty – to the *neighbour* whom we love (through giving), to the *God* on whom we depend (through prayer) and to *ourselves* with whom we exercise discipline and self-control (through fasting).

The difference between Pharisaic piety and Christian piety was not, therefore, in what they did, but rather in how and why they did it, and in its consequences.

This is so important, and the distinctions Jesus made are so relevant to religious practice today, that we will study these verses more carefully.

The pattern of each of the three paragraphs is the same. Jesus contrasts first two possible ways (Pharisaic and Christian) of practising the piety in question, then the two motives behind them and finally the two resulting rewards.

Alternative forms of religion

He begins with the alternative forms of piety, namely the ostentatious and the secret. Jesus describes the religious display of the Pharisees in vivid, even humorous, detail. When they are about to give to the needy, they give a loud trumpet blast to draw attention to their charity (v. 2). When they pray, they choose a conspicuous place either in the synagogue or at a street corner (v. 5). When they fast, they disfigure their faces, making themselves dirty and dishevelled, perhaps smearing themselves with ashes so as to look pale through their strict diet, and they look dismal as well (v. 16).

It is easy to poke fun at them – but our Christian Pharisaism is not so amusing. We may not blow trumpets, but we like to see our name on lists of donors. We may not pray on street corners, but we like to gain a reputation for our disciplined life of prayer. We may not put on sackcloth and ashes, but, if we ever did fast, we would certainly want to make sure everybody knew about it.

Christian piety, on the other hand, is secret piety. 'Secret' is the key word in this whole section, being repeated six times. Thus (vv. 3, 4), when we give to the needy, not only are we not to tell others about our Christian giving, we are not even to let our left hand know what our right hand is doing. That is, we are not to dwell on it in our own mind in a spirit of self-congratulation. Instead, our giving is to be, in every way, unself-conscious.

When we pray (v. 6), we are to go into our room and close the door, not only against distraction and interruption, but also against all human spectators. Then in privacy and secrecy we are to pray to our Father 'who is in that secret place'.

Similarly, when we fast (vv. 17, 18), Jesus tells us to 'put oil on your head and wash your face'. This does not mean that we are to do anything unusual to our head and face. Christian piety does not put hypocrisy into reverse and put on an artificially smiling face instead of a dismal one. No. We are, as it were, to wash our face and brush our hair in the ordinary way. Then, seeing nothing abnormal about our appearance or routine, nobody will guess what is going on in secret.

In each case showing off is the stock-in-trade of the Pharisee; Christian piety is practised in secret.

Alternative motives for religion

Behind this difference in form and practice there lies a difference in motive. The reason the Pharisees parade their piety in public is to draw attention to themselves and win the admiration of others. The Pharisees were essentially people-pleasers. They practised their piety 'before others' in order to be 'seen by others' (vv. 1, 5, 16) and gave to the needy in order to be 'honoured by others' (v. 2).

The word Jesus gave to this religious show was 'hypocrisy'. When he told his disciples to 'Be on your guard against the yeast of the Pharisees and Sadducees',[23] it was to this as much as to their teaching that he was referring. The *hypokritēs* is the actor, playing a part on the stage, pretending to be someone they are not. They are wearing a mask. Their appearance is not the reality, but a disguise. And hypocrites in religion are the same. They are playing a game of 'let's pretend', and they do it in order to be seen by others. The Greek word for this is *theathēnai*, meaning that they are giving a theatrical display before an audience. It is all done for show, for applause.

The tragedy is that giving and praying and fasting simply cannot be treated in this way. For they are *real* activities, involving *real* people. If we turn them into a pretence, we actually destroy them. The purpose of giving to the needy is to relieve distress. The purpose of prayer to enjoy communion with God. The purpose of fasting is to discipline ourselves for some spiritual good. But hypocrites are not interested in the real purpose of these practices; they exploit them to gratify their own vanity. They actually use God and their fellow human beings (or practices intended to honour God and serve others) to pander to their own conceit. They turn religion and charity into a parade to boost their own ego. It is hard to exaggerate just how wicked this is.

If the motive behind Pharisaic piety is selfish (the advancement of their own glory), the motive behind Christian piety is godly (the advancement of the glory of God). To begin with, the Christian recognizes that giving, praying and fasting are important in their own right. They are intended to express a genuine desire to serve others, to seek God and to discipline self. In one sense we have no need or wish to look further than this. But there is something further to be said. For although, as we have seen, these three practices relate obviously to others, God and self – yet the Christian also relates them all to God. We know that everything we do as Christians is done to please, honour and glorify God. So, although we are to give and pray and fast in secret so far as other people are concerned, we do not do these things in secret so far as God is concerned. On the contrary, 'the secret place' in which we are to give and pray and fast is the very place which God sees and where God is.

It is a beautiful truth: to practise our religion *before others* is guaranteed to degrade it. But to practise it *before God* is equally certain to enrich it. It is the only way to ensure that it will be real, genuine and true. Why is this? Partly because of who and what God is, and partly because this God 'sees' – not the outward appearance which is all other people see but the heart, not the deed itself only but the thoughts and the motives which lie behind the deed. So to live and act in the presence of God ensures reality, while to practise our piety before others is simply to play games.

I think a short digression is necessary at this stage. Some people are puzzled by the seeming contradiction between this ban against practising our piety before others to be seen by them (Matthew 6:1) and the earlier command to let our light shine before others that they may see our good deeds (5:16). Are we to live our Christian lives before others to be seen by them or not? Let me make three points in order to clarify this.

First, these two verses refer to different aspects of our Christian life. The acts of 'piety' which are not to be done before others to be seen by them are the practices of giving, praying and fasting, which can and should be secret. But the 'light' which we are to allow to shine before others to be seen, on the other hand, is our good deeds; these are works of mercy like feeding the hungry, clothing the naked and nursing the sick, which clearly cannot be hidden from those who benefit from them.

Secondly, the two verses are directed against different failures. It is the sin of cowardice which made Jesus say 'let your light shine before others', but the sin of vanity which made him warn his followers 'not to practise your righteousness in front of others'. In other words, we are to 'show when tempted to *hide*' and 'hide when tempted to *show*'.[24]

Thirdly, despite these differences, the ultimate goal of both the ban and the command is the same, namely the greater glory of God. Our piety must be secret and our good works public so that people may glorify our heavenly Father rather than us.

Returning from this digression, we are ready now to consider the alternative rewards for piety.

Alternative rewards for religion

What reward do the Pharisees get for their vain display? The obvious answer is 'none': 'you will have no reward from your Father in heaven' (v. 1). But this states that they will receive no reward from *God*. It does not say that they will get no reward at all. As a matter of fact, they will be rewarded. They will get the reward they want – no more and no less – praise from other people. What reward is an actor looking for once the play is finished? The applause of the audience. What reward does the religious play-actor get? The same: applause! But once the applause has died down, there is no further reward to come. This is the thrust of the solemn words Jesus repeated three times: 'Truly I tell you, they have received their reward *in full*'

(vv. 2, 5, 16). The verb was commonly used at that time for giving a receipt, indicating that there is nothing else to pay.

Christians, on the other hand, since they give and pray and fast in secret, neither expect nor receive a reward from others. But Jesus is clear: their heavenly Father will reward them. Jesus affirmed it three times: 'Your Father, who sees what is done in secret, will reward you' (vv. 4, 6, 18). Some Christians draw back from this. They say that they don't want any reward; they even dismiss the promise. But Christian disciples should not treat the teaching of their Lord and Master in such a high-handed way. If Jesus said it, we may be sure that he meant it.

So what did he mean? What is the nature of the reward? There is nothing in the context to suggest that the promised reward will be presented at some future 'prize-giving'. Since hypocrites receive their reward there and then, I am inclined to think that Christians do also. May it not be an immediate and spiritual reward? The rewards which God gives to those who are sincere in the practice of their religion are rich indeed. To give secretly is to share with God the secret discovery that 'it is more blessed to give than to receive'.[25] To pray in the secret place is to find God there, waiting to satisfy their hunger with good things, to refresh their spirit and renew their strength. To fast in secret is to be rewarded by an increasing self-control, and by the joy, peace and freedom which flow from it.

Modern Pharisaism and its remedy

We have seen the stark contrast which Jesus paints in the Sermon on the Mount between Pharisaic and Christian piety. They assume different forms (the ostentatious and the secret), are directed by different motives (glorification of self and the glory of God) and receive different rewards (the applause of other people and the blessing of God). Nothing could indicate more clearly the far-reaching influence of false, Pharisaic ambition, namely to love the praise of others more than the praise of God. If it prevented their conversion, silenced their witness and spoiled their social behaviour, it entirely ruined their practice of piety.

The same Pharisaic spirit still haunts us today. It is easy to be critical of those Christ was dealing with back then and miss the reflection of their vanity in ourselves. Yet this yearning to be praised by others is deeply embedded in our fallen nature. It seems to be a devilish distortion of our basic psychological need to be wanted and to be loved. We hunger for applause, we fish for compliments, we thrive on flattery, we want to be congratulated by others. We are simply not content with God's approval now or with the prospect of his 'Well done, good and faithful servant' on the last day.

The answer lies, Jesus suggested, in recognizing that this quest for glory is a form of idolatry. 'You accept glory from one another,' he said to his Jewish contemporaries, 'but do not seek the glory that comes from *the only God*.'[26] His description of the Father in this context as 'the only God' was deliberate and significant. He was implying that the giving and the receiving of 'glory' are for God alone. It's precisely because he is God that glory (or praise) is due to him alone and must be sought from him alone. Once we recognize that glory is God's both to give and to receive, then we see that to replace him in either must be idolatrous. It is to take away from God the glory which is his alone. Which is, in effect, to deny that God is God.

But why is this?

Glory is due *to* God alone because he is our Creator. The source of our being is God. Both the material and the spiritual creation owe their origin to his will and power because 'it is he who made us, and not we ourselves'.[27] Our very life is in God's hand. Physically, he 'gives everyone life and breath and every-thing else'.[28] Spiritually also, through Christ, he 'gives life to whom he is pleased to give it'.[29] Christians, then, who are both physically and spiritually alive, acknowledge their complete dependence of body and soul on the Lord, the Life-giver. We join with Paul in saying that 'by the grace of God I am what I am'.[30] This is not pious make-believe, but simple fact. Humility is nothing but the truth.

Glory also comes *from* God alone because he alone is our Judge. Jesus taught this too: 'I am not seeking glory for myself,' he said, 'but there is one who seeks it, and he is the judge.'[31] It is to God that we are ultimately responsible and must explain ourselves. It is to him alone, therefore, that we should look for approval. Besides, he is uniquely capable of true judgment because he is just and merciful, completely impartial and knows the secrets of every heart. If, therefore, we either receive glory from other people or take it upon ourselves to give glory to them, we are usurping a right that is God's alone and seating ourselves on his throne of judgment.

The apostle Paul is a good example of one who looked for glory from God alone. He had learned to resist human flattery and criticism, not because he was insensitive (far from it), but because he knew he had a heavenly Master and Judge to whom he was responsible and before whom his heart was an open book. He lived in the presence of God. Again and again in his Epistles he called God to witness. As a servant of Christ and steward of God's revealed secrets, he knew he was required to be faithful to him and him alone. So he could say, 'I care very little if I am judged by you or by any human court; indeed, I do not even judge myself. My conscience is clear, but that does not make me innocent. It is the Lord who judges me. Therefore judge nothing before the appointed time; wait until the Lord comes.

He will bring to light what is hidden in darkness and will expose the motives of the heart. At that time each will receive their praise from God.'[32]

Every sin is a surrender to the basic temptation to become like God. It is an act of rebellion against the 'Godness' of God, a person's proud unwillingness simply to be what they are and let God be God. The human desire for glory is a particularly serious form of sin because it denies God his unique glory as both Creator and Judge.

It is only when we humble ourselves and acknowledge that God is God, our Creator and our Judge, our Beginning from whom we come and our End to whom we go that the Pharisaism within us will surrender to true Christianity. Then we shall no longer live horizontally like the Pharisees (seeking glory from, and giving glory to, other people) but vertically (recognizing God as the sole source and recipient of glory). We shall love the glory of God more than the glory of human beings. Delivered from the weight and oppression of self-centredness, we shall begin to experience heaven on earth, the life with God's eternal throne at the centre.

Postscript:

Jesus, our Teacher and Lord

If I thought that being an evangelical Christian involved a party loyalty which took priority over allegiance to Christ, I would give up being an evangelical immediately. The very idea of putting Christ in second place to a party is abhorrent to me. My sincerely held belief as an evangelical is that it is my very loyalty to Christ which requires me to hold evangelical views.

This, at any rate, has been the theme of this book. We have studied the major controversies of Christ and have tried to isolate the issues which he focused on when talking with the Pharisees and Sadducees. He put the Sadducees' error down to their ignorance of the power of God. When it came to the Pharisees, he insisted that our authority is to be found in God's Word alone (without adding human traditions) and that our acceptance comes from God's mercy alone (without adding human merit). He taught that the morality and the worship which please God are those of the heart, inward rather than outward. He emphasized that our responsibility as Christians is to be involved in the world, not to withdraw from it, and that our overriding Christian ambition should not be to seek our own glory, but the glory of God.

These issues emerge plainly from the debates of Jesus with the religious leaders of his day. And each debate has continued into our own day. Not one of them is dead. The only question is whether we identify ourselves with him or with those he criticized, whether our Christianity is in fact genuinely Christian or a modern version of Pharisaism or Sadduceeism.

In this connection I have myself been helped by some words Jesus spoke in the Upper Room just after he had washed the apostles' feet. When he had returned to his place, he said to them, 'You call me "Teacher" and "Lord," and rightly so, for that is what I am. Now that I, your Lord and Teacher, have washed your feet, you also should wash one another's feet.'[1]

'Teacher' and 'Lord' were polite forms of address used in conversation with rabbis which the apostles used in addressing Jesus. What he was now saying is that in his case they were more than courtesy titles; they expressed a fundamental reality. I am in fact, he declared, what you call me in title.

This verse tells us something very important both about Christ and about Christians.

What it tells us about Christ concerns his awareness of himself as Son of God. Though just a peasant from Galilee, a carpenter by trade and a preacher by vocation, he claimed to be the teacher and the lord of all. He said he had authority over them to tell them what to believe and to do. This is a clear (if indirect) claim to divinity, for no mere human being can ever exercise lordship over the minds and wills of others. More than this, in supporting his claim he showed no sign of mental unbalance. On the contrary, he had just got up from supper, wrapped a towel around himself, poured water into a basin, knelt down and washed their feet. He who said he was their teacher and lord humbled himself to be their servant. And it is this paradoxical combination of lordship and service, authority and humility, lofty claims and lowly conduct, which represents the strongest evidence that (in John's words in this passage) 'he had come from God and was returning to God' (v. 3).

Secondly, the same verse reveals the proper relationship of Christians to Christ. This is not only that of sinners to their Saviour, but also of students to their Teacher and servants to their Lord. Indeed, these things are inseparably bound together. He is 'our Lord and Saviour Jesus Christ'. What, then, are the implications of saying that Jesus is our Teacher and Lord?

Of course, everybody agrees that Jesus of Nazareth was a great teacher. Many are prepared to go at least as far as Nicodemus and call him 'a teacher who has come from God'.[2] Furthermore, it is clear that one of the most striking things about his teaching was the authority with which he gave it. He did not hesitate. He never spoke tentatively, diffidently, apologetically. No. He knew what he wanted to say, and he said it with quiet, simple confidence. This is what impressed people so much. As they listened to him, we read that 'they were amazed at his teaching, because his words had authority'.[3]

There is only one logical conclusion from all this. If the Jesus who taught like this was indeed the Son of God made flesh, we must bow to his authority and accept his teaching. We must allow our opinions to be moulded by his opinions, our views to be modified by his views. And this includes his uncomfortable and unfashionable teaching, some of which we have been considering in this book. Like his view of God as a supreme, spiritual, personal, powerful Being, the Creator, Controller, Father and King, and of human beings as made in the image of God but now fallen, with hearts so corrupt as to be the source of all the evil things they think, say and do. Again, as we have seen, he taught the divine origin, supreme authority and complete sufficiency of Scripture as God's Word written, whose primary purpose is to direct sinners to their Saviour in order to find life. He also taught (although we have not considered this) the fact of divine judgment as a process of sifting which begins in this life and is settled at death. He confirmed that our final destinations are the awful alternatives of heaven and hell, adding that these destinations are unalterable with a great chasm fixed between them.

Yet these traditional Christian truths are being called in question today. The independent, personal, transcendent being of God, the essential sinfulness of human beings, the inspiration and authority of Scripture, the solemn, eternal realities of heaven and hell – all this (and more) is being not only questioned but in many places actually abandoned. Our simple claim is that no-one can abandon such plain gospel truths as these and still call Jesus 'Teacher'.

Of course, there have been plenty of other religious teachers. But Jesus went further, claiming also to be Lord. Teachers instruct their students. They may even plead with them to follow their teaching. But they cannot command agreement, however, still less obedience. Yet this right was exercised by Jesus as Lord. 'If you love me,' he said, 'keep my commands.'[4] 'Anyone who loves their father or mother . . . son or daughter more than me is not worthy of me.'[5] What he asked from his disciples was nothing less than their supreme love and loyalty.

So Christians look to Jesus Christ both as their Teacher and their Lord, their Teacher to instruct them and their Lord to command them. We are proud to be more than his pupils; we are his servants as well. We recognize his right to lay upon us duties and obligations: 'Now that I, your Lord and Teacher, have washed your feet, you also should wash one another's feet.'[6]

This 'should' we accept from the authority of Jesus. We desire not only to submit our minds to his teaching but our wills to his obedience. And this is what he expected: 'Very truly I tell you, no servant [literally 'slave'] is greater than his master.'[7] He therefore calls us to adopt his standards, which are completely different from the world's, and to assess greatness not in terms of success but of service, not of self-promotion but of self-sacrifice.

Because we are fallen and proud human beings, we find this part of Christian discipleship very difficult. We like to have our own opinions (especially if they are different from everybody else's) and to air them rather pompously in conversation. We also like to live our own lives, set our own standards and go our own way. In brief, we like to be our own master, our own teacher and lord. People sometimes defend this position by saying that it would be impossible to surrender our independence of thought – and that even if it were possible it would be wrong. This is the mood of the age, both in the world and in the church. We are not prepared either to believe or do anything simply because some 'authority' requires it. But what if that authority is Christ's and if Christ's authority is God's? What then? The only Christian answer is that we submit, humbly, gladly, and with the full consent of our mind and will.

But is this in fact what we do? It is quite easy to test ourselves. What is our authority for believing what we believe and doing what we do? Is it what we think and what we want? Or is it what Professor So-and-so has written, what Bishop Such-and-such has said? Or is it what Jesus Christ has made known, either directly or through his apostles?

We may not particularly like what he taught about God and humanity, Scripture and salvation, worship and morality, duty and destiny, heaven and hell. But can we dare to prefer our own opinions and standards *and still call ourselves Christian*? Or do we presume to say that he did not know what he was talking about, that he was a weak and fallible teacher, or that he adjusted his views to match those of his contemporaries even though he knew them to be mistaken? Such suggestions are appallingly insulting to the honour of the Son of God.

Of course we have a responsibility to grapple with Christ's teaching, its perplexities and problems, seeking to understand it and to relate it to our own situation. But ultimately the question which faces the church is very simple: is Jesus Christ Lord or not? And if he is Lord, is he Lord of all? The lordship of Jesus must be allowed to extend over every aspect of the lives of those who claim that 'Jesus is Lord', including their minds and their wills. Why should these be excluded from his otherwise universal dominion? No-one is truly converted who is not intellectually and morally converted. And no-one is intellectually converted if they have not submitted their mind to the mind of the Lord Christ, nor morally converted if they have not submitted their will to the will of the Lord Christ.

The thing is that such submission is not bondage but freedom – freedom from the inconsistencies of self, the fashions of the world and the trends of the church. It spells freedom from the shifting sands of subjectivity, freedom to exercise our minds and our wills as God intended them to be exercised, not in rebellion against him but in submission to him.

I do not hesitate to say that these are the kind of people Jesus Christ is looking for in the church today, people who will take him seriously as their Teacher and Lord, not paying lip-service to these titles ('Why do you call me, "Lord, Lord," and do not do what I say?'),[8] but actually taking his yoke upon them, in order to learn from him and to 'take captive every thought to make it obedient to Christ'.[9]

This will involve for us, first, a greater commitment to study. We can't believe or obey Jesus Christ unless we know what he taught. One of the church's most urgent needs today is for its ordinary members to have a much closer familiarity with the Bible. How lovingly the student should prize the teaching of such a Master!

It will also involve a greater commitment to humility. By nature we hate authority and love independence. We think that having an independent judgment and demonstrating an independent spirit is great. Which is quite true if we mean that we don't want to be sheep who follow the crowd, or reeds shaken by the winds of public opinion. But to be independent of Jesus Christ is not a virtue but a vice – indeed a very great sin in one who claims to be a Christian. Christians are not free to disagree with Christ or to disobey Christ. On the contrary, they are really keen to shape both their thinking and their living to the teaching of Christ.

And the good sense of this Christian humility lies in the identity of the Teacher. If Jesus of Nazareth were merely human, it would be ludicrous to submit our minds and our wills to him like this. But it's because he is the Son of God that is ludicrous *not* to do so. Submission to him is just plain Christian common sense and duty.

I believe that Jesus Christ is addressing the church of our day with the same words: 'You call me "Teacher" and "Lord," and rightly so, for that is what I am.' My prayer is that, having listened to his words, we will not want to use these merely as courtesy titles, but give him the honour he deserves by our humble belief and wholehearted obedience.

Notes

A. A call for clarity

1. Hebrews 1:1–2.
2. 1 John 3:2.
3. Deuteronomy 3:24.
4. 1 Corinthians 13:11.
5. Acts 1:7.
6. Deuteronomy 29:29.
7. James S. Stewart, *Heralds of God* (Hodder and Stoughton, 1946), p. 210.
8. Ephesians 4:14.
9. 2 Timothy 3:7.
10. Titus 1:9.
11. 1 Corinthians 13:7.
12. 2 Timothy 2:23.
13. Philippians 1:7.
14. John 14:6; 18:37; 8:31, 32.
15. E.g. Matthew 7:15–20; Mark 13:5, 6, 21–23; Luke 12:1.
16. Matthew 15:14; 23:16, 19, 24, 26; 7:15; 23:27; Luke 11:44; Matthew 12:34; 23:33.
17. Jude 1:3.
18. 1 John 2:22.
19. Galatians 1:6–9.
20. Ephesians 4:15.
21. 1 Timothy 3:15.

B. Why 'evangelical'?

1. From an address given to the Fellowship of Evangelical Churchmen on 20 March 1961, and subsequently published with the title *The Theological Challenge to Evangelicalism Today*.

2. Acts 20:27.
3. 2 Thessalonians 3:6.
4. 2 Thessalonians 3:14.
5. 2 John 1:9.
6. 2 Thessalonians 2:15; cf. 3:6; Romans 16:7.
7. 1 Corinthians 15:1, 2; cf. 16:13; Philippians 4:9;
    Colossians. 2:6.
8. Galatians 1:8, 9.
9. 1 Timothy 6:20; cf. 4:6.
10. 2 Timothy 1:13, 14; cf. 2:2.
11. 2 Timothy 3:14; cf. Titus 1:9.
12. 1 Peter 1:23–25.
13. 2 Peter 1:12–15.
14. Hebrews 2:1.
15. Hebrews 13:7, 9.
16. 1 John 2:7.
17. 1 John 2:24, 26; cf. 3:11; 4:6; 2 John 5, 6.
18. Jude 1:3.
19. Revelation 2:24, 25.
20. 1 John 2:7–8.
21. Psalm 40:3.
22. P. T. Forsyth, *Positive Preaching and the Modern Mind*
    (Independent Press, 1907), p. 60.
23. *Works*, III (Oxford, 1843), p. 26.
24. James Clarke, *A Commentary on St. Paul's Epistle to the
    Galatians* (1953), p. 53.
25. *Works*, vol. I, pp. 30f.
26. From a letter dated July 1825 and quoted in Handley C. G.
    Moule, *Charles Simeon* (1892; IVP edition, 1965), pp. 77, 78.
27. William Carus (ed.), *Memoirs of the Life of the Rev. Charles
    Simeon* (Hatchard, 1847), p. 180.

1. Religion: Natural or supernatural?

1. Acts 5:17.

2. Article 'Pharisees' by Hugh M. Scott, in Hastings'
   Dictionary of Christ and the Gospels (vol. II, 1908), p. 351.
3. From *The Works of Flavius Josephus*, trans. William Whiston
   (1737): *The Antiquities of the Jews* xviii.1.3, 4 and *The Wars
   of the Jews* ii.8.14.
4. Mark 12:18.
5. Acts 23:8.
6. Mark 12:19.
7. Mark 12:20–23.
8. Luke 10:26.
9. Mark 12:26.
10. Mark 10:3.
11. Genesis 17:7.
12. Hebrews 11:13, 16.
13. Luke 20:38.
14. Luke 20:37.
15. *Apocalypse of Baruch* 49:2, 3; 50:1, 2.
16. E. Earle Ellis, *The Gospel of Luke* (*The Century Bible*)
    (Nelson, 1966), p. 236.
17. Luke 20:34–36.
18. 1 Corinthians 15:52.
19. Genesis 9:7.
20. 1 Corinthians 15:37–38, 42–44.
21. Quoted by Professor C. A. Coulson in *Science and Christian
    Belief* (OUP, 1955; Fontana edition, 1958), pp. 32, 33.
22. C. A. Coulson, *Science and Christian Belief* (OUP, 1955;
    Fontana, 1958), p. 41.
23. Ibid., p. 27.
24. J. Huxley, *Religion Without Revelation* (Ernest Benn, 1927),
    p. 12.
25. Donald M. MacKay, *Science and Christian Faith Today*
    (Falcon, 1960), pp. 3, 5.
26. Huxley, *Religion Without Revelation*, p. 58.
27. Jeremiah 23:24.

28. Hebrews 1:3.
29. Colossians 1:17.
30. Psalm 24:1.
31. Genesis 8:22.
32. Matthew 5:45.
33. Acts 17:25.
34. Acts 17:28.
35. Genesis 3:19.
36. Ephesians 1:19–20.
37. Philippians 3:21.
38. 1 Corinthians 15:49.
39. John 5:24–25.
40. Ephesians 2:1, 4–6.
41. Colossians 3:1.
42. Luke 9:22.
43. John 5:21.
44. Ephesians 1:19.
45. Philippians 3:10.
46. Philippians 3:21.

2. Authority: Tradition or Scripture?
1. Matthew 16:6.
2. Matthew 21:23.
3. Josephus, *Antiquities* xiii. 10.6.
4. A. Edersheim, *The Life and Times of Jesus the Messiah* (Longmans, 1883), vol. II, p. 15.
5. Quoted in Alan Cole, *The Epistle of Paul to the Galatians* (Tyndale New Testament Commentaries) (Tyndale Press, 1965), p. 50.
6. Mark 7:1–13. An abbreviated version of the same debate occurs in Matthew 15:1–9.
7. 2 Timothy 2:2.
8. 2 Thessalonians 3:6.
9. Henry Alford, *The Greek Testament* (Rivington, 1849–61).

10. H. B. Swete, *The Gospel According to St. Mark* (Macmillan, 1898), Comment on Mark 7:7.

11. Exodus 20:12.

12. Cf. Exodus 21:17.

13. Matthew 15:2–3.

14. C. E. B. Cranfield, *The Gospel According to St. Mark* (*Cambridge Greek Testament*) (CUP, 1959), pp. 233, 236.

15. Quoted by Swete in his comment on Mark 7:9.

16. Philip Schaff, *The Creeds of Christendom*, 6th edition (Harper, 1931), vol. II, p. 80.

17. Cranmer, *Works*, I, p. 52.

18. *Sermons of Hugh Latimer*, Parker Society Edition (CUP, 1844), pp. 70, 71.

19. Westminster Confession I.6.

20. Hodder and Stoughton, 1901.

3. The Bible: End or means?

1. John 5:39, 40.

2. John 10:35.

3. Matthew 5:18.

4. E.g. Matthew 4:4, 7, 10.

5. Daniel 7:13.

6. E.g. Isaiah 42:1.

7. Luke 2:49.

8. Mark 8:31.

9. Matthew 26:24.

10. Luke 18:31.

11. Philippians 2:8.

12. Matthew 26:53–54.

13. Luke 24:25–27.

14. Matthew 15:7.

15. Hebrews 1:1.

16. 2 Peter 1:21.

17. Romans 3:2.

18. Psalm 147:20.
19. Psalm 119:162.
20. Psalm 19:10.
21. See Acts 17:10–12.
22. Galatians 3:24.
23. Luke 24:27.
24. Matthew 13:16–17.
25. John 20:31.
26. 2 Timothy 3:15.
27. Dr J. I. Packer in an article on the sacraments published in *Church Gazette* (September/October 1962).
28. Acts 18:24.

4. Salvation: Merit or mercy?

1. Jude 1:3.
2. Romans 6:10.
3. 1 Peter 3:18.
4. Hebrews 9:26–28.
5. Matthew 16:17.
6. Galatians 1:15–16.
7. 2 Corinthians 4:6.
8. 1 Corinthians 12:3.
9. Ephesians 2:8–10.
10. 2 Corinthians 5:18.
11. Luke 18:9–14.
12. Luke 10:29.
13. Luke 16:15.
14. Proverbs 17:15.
15. Exodus 23:7.
16. Romans 4:5.
17. Hugh M. Scott, 'Pharisees', in Hastings' *Dictionary of Christ and the Gospels* (Clark, vol. II, 1908), pp. 351–356; cf. John 7:49.
18. *Psalms of Solomon* 9:7–15; 13:9; 14:1–6.

19. Alfred Edersheim, *The Life and Times of Jesus the Messiah* (Longman, 1883), vol. I, p. 540.
20. 1 Timothy 1:15.
21. Ezra 9:6.
22. Matthew 21:31.
23. Exodus 34:6.
24. Matthew 18:21–35.
25. John 4:10.
26. John 6:27.
27. Philippians 3:3.
28. Philippians 3:4–6.
29. Philippians 3:7–9.
30. Matthew 20:28.
31. Matthew 26:28.
32. John 10:11, 18.
33. John 12:24, 32.
34. Galatians 3:1.
35. John 3:14–15.
36. John 6:53–54.
37. Acts 2:38.
38. John 6:54.
39. 1 Peter 2:5, 9; Revelation 1:6.
40. Hebrews 10:19.
41. 1 Peter 2:5; Hebrews 13:15; Romans 12:1.
42. Jeremiah 6:14.
43. Romans 3:26.
44. Romans 6:1.
45. Romans 6:2.
46. James 2:18.
47. Galatians 5:6.
48. Galatians 2:21.
49. James 3:9.
50. Ephesians 4:24; Colossians 3:10.
51. Romans 3:27.

52. 1 Corinthians 1:31.

53. Revelation 3:17.

54. *Commentary on Galatians* (James Clarke, 1953), p. 143.

55. From the 'Homily on Salvation' (1547) in *Book of Homilies and Canons*, pp. 25, 26. Compare Article XI, *Of the Justification of Man*: 'We are accounted righteous before God, only for the merit of our Lord and Saviour Jesus Christ by Faith, and not for our own works or deservings: wherefore, that we are justified by Faith only is a most wholesome Doctrine, and very full of comfort . . .'

5. Morality: Outward or inward?

1. Mark 7:1–23.

2. Scott, p. 351.

3. Scott, p. 354.

4. Edersheim, vol. II, pp. 9–14.

5. Matthew 15:12.

6. Matthew 10:31.

7. John 10:11.

8. Psalm 53:3.

9. E.g. Matthew 12:39.

10. Matthew 7:11.

11. Jeremiah 17:9.

12. Matthew 7:16–20.

13. Matthew 12:34.

14. Matthew 12:33.

15. Luke 6:45.

16. Mark 15:38.

17. Ezekiel 36:26–27.

18. Jeremiah 31:33.

19. Galatians 5:22–23.

20. John 15:5.

21. Bishop J. C. Ryle, *Knots Untied* (Thynne, 1871), pp. 4, 5.

22. See Amos 1:3 – 2:5.
23. Ephesians 6:4.
24. Romans 13:1ff.; 1 Peter 2:13, 14.
25. Luke 16:15.
26. Matthew 5:20.
27. Philippians 3:6.
28. Matthew 19:3–9.
29. Matthew 5:38.
30. Matthew 5:38–42.
31. Matthew 5:43–48.
32. Matthew 5:33–37.
33. Matthew 5:21–30.
34. Romans 13:8–10.
35. Romans 8:3.
36. Romans 6:14.
37. Galatians 5:18.
38. Romans 8:4.
39. Jeremiah 31:33; 2 Corinthians 3:3.
40. *The True Bounds of Christian Freedom* (1645) quoted by E. F. Kevan in *Keep His Commandments* (Tyndale Press, 1964), pp. 28, 29.
41. Galatians 6:15.
42. 1 Corinthians 7:19.
43. 1 John 3:4.
44. 1 John 2:3–5; 3:4–10, 22–24; 5:1–5, 18.
45. Psalm 119:97.
46. Romans 7:22.
47. Psalm 19:8.
48. John 18:28.
49. Matthew 9:13; 12:7.
50. Matthew 12:1ff.
51. Matthew 12:9ff.
52. Matthew 12:7.
53. Luke 13:15.

54. Mark 3:4.
55. Matthew 9:9–13.

6. Worship: Lips or heart?
1. E.g. Isaiah 1:12–14; Amos 5:21–24.
2. Matthew 15:7–9.
3. Matthew 6:6.
4. E.g. Proverbs 2:2; 23:15.
5. Acts 16:14.
6. Acts 17:23.
7. John 4:22–23.
8. Revelation 22:3–4.
9. 1 Corinthians 13:12.
10. John 4:20–24.
11. 1 Kings 8:27.
12. Jeremiah 31:33; Ezekiel 37:27; cf. 2 Corinthians 6:16.
13. Matthew 18:20.
14. Matthew 28:20.
15. Hebrews 12:22–24.
16. Psalm 51:16–17.
17. Hebrews 12:28–29.
18. Philippians 3:3.
19. Ephesians 2:18.
20. Romans 8:26.
21. Romans 8:15.
22. John 4:16–18.
23. Psalm 24:3–4.
24. Proverbs 15:8.
25. 1 Samuel 15:22.
26. Amos 5:21–24.
27. Isaiah 1:11–17.
28. Amos 2:8.
29. Mark 12:40.
30. 1 John 1:5–6, 2:4, 9.

7. Responsibility: Withdrawal or involvement?

1. Luke 15:1–2.
2. Matthew 23:15.
3. Exodus 6:7.
4. Exodus 19:5–6.
5. 2 Chronicles 36:16.
6. Nehemiah 10:28.
7. Isaiah 4:2–6; 49:6, 8; Luke 2:32.
8. John 7:48-49.
9. Matthew 18:17.
10. E.g. Luke 5:29–32; 15:1, 20.
11. Luke 15:1.
12. F. W. Farrar, *The Life of Christ* (Cassell, 1874), p. 448.
13. Mark 10:14–16.
14. Mark 10:46–52.
15. John 4:27.
16. Luke 7:36–50.
17. John 4:9.
18. Mark 1:41.
19. Luke 4:40.
20. Mark 5:25–34.
21. Mark 5:21–24, 35–43.
22. Luke 18:11.
23. Luke 19:7.
24. Luke 5:29–30.
25. Luke 19:10.
26. Mark 2:17.
27. Luke 15:2.
28. Luke 15:1–7.
29. C. G. Montefiore, *The Synoptic Gospels* (London, 1927), vol. I, p. cxviii and vol. II, p. 520. Quoted by S. C. Neill in *Christian Faith Today* (Pelican, 1955), p. 165.
30. Luke 15:8–10.
31. Luke 15:11–32.

32. Luke 15:20.
33. Abbé G. Michonneau, *Revolution in a City Parish* (Blackfriars, 1949), p. 21.
34. Galatians 3:28.
35. 1 John 2:15–17; Romans 12:2; James 1:27.
36. John 17:15.
37. 1 Timothy 1:15.
38. Luke 24:47.
39. *The Uppsala Report 1968* edited by Norman Goodall (World Council of Churches, 1968), pp. 317, 318 and 320.
40. Luke 7:34.
41. John 20:21.
42. *Witness in Six Continents*, ed. R. K. Orchard (Edinburgh House Press, 1964), pp. 151, 158.

8. Ambition: Our glory or God's?

1. John 12:43.
2. John 8:50.
3. John 7:18.
4. John 12:28.
5. John 17:4.
6. *Defence of the True and Catholic Doctrine of the Lord's Supper*, 1550, in his *Works*, Book V, ch. 1, p. 232.
7. Mark 10:42–45.
8. E.g. 1 Thessalonians 5:12, 13; 1 Timothy 3:5; Hebrews 13:7, 17.
9. 1 Peter 5:3.
10. Matthew 23:8–10.
11. See 1 Corinthians 1:10–17.
12. 1 Corinthians 3:21–23.
13. *Works* (St. Louis edition), X. 370.
14. Letter to the Editor of the *Christian Observer* in 1803. This and the following quotation appear in Michael Hennell, *John Venn and the Clapham Sect* (Lutterworth, 1958), pp. 262, 263.

15. John 5:41.
16. John 5:44.
17. Proverbs 29:25.
18. Mark 8:38.
19. John 12:42–43.
20. Colossians 3:22.
21. Galatians 1:10.
22. Matthew 23:5–7.
23. Matthew 16:6.
24. A. B. Bruce, *The Synoptic Gospels* (*The Expositor's Greek Testament*) (Hodder and Stoughton, 1897). Comment on Matthew 6:1.
25. Acts 20:35.
26. John 5:44.
27. Psalm 100:3, RSV margin.
28. Acts 17:25.
29. John 5:21.
30. 1 Corinthians 15:10.
31. John 8:50.
32. 1 Corinthians 4:3–5.

Postscript: Jesus, our Teacher and Lord

1. John 13:13–14.
2. John 3:2.
3. Luke 4:32.
4. John 14:15.
5. Matthew 10:37.
6. John 13:14.
7. John 13:16.
8. Luke 6:46.
9. 2 Corinthians 10:5.

John Stott: A Timeline

April 27, 1921	Born in London
February 13, 1938	Conversion after hearing Eric (Bash) Nash preach
1938–1940	Decides to be ordained
October 1940	Enters Trinity College, Cambridge
June 1943	Graduates with double first
October 1944	Graduate studies in theology at Ridley Hall, Cambridge
December 21, 1945	Ordained deacon in St. Paul's Cathedral; becomes curate at All Souls
September 26, 1950	Instituted as rector of All Souls parish
January 1954	First book, *Men with a Message*, published
1954	Supports Billy Graham in Harringay Crusade
November 1955	Assistant missioner to Billy Graham at Cambridge
1956	Frances Whitehead appointed secretary
November 1956	Sails from Southampton for missions in the US and Canada
1958	*Basic Christianity* published. Missions in Australia
June 1959	Appointed chaplain to the Queen
Spring 1962	Second visit to Africa Visits to Keswick Convention begin
December 1964	First of six visits to Urbana Student Missions Convention, University of Illinois
October 18, 1966	Public disagreement with Dr Martyn Lloyd-Jones
April 1967	First National Evangelical Congress at Keele University
1968	Begins editing and contributing to The Bible Speaks Today series
December 1970	Speaks for third time at Urbana Student Missions Convention
April 1971	Begins to divert book royalties to Evangelical Literature Trust

Autumn 1972	Guest lecturer at Trinity Evangelical Divinity School, Deerfield, Illinois
January 1974	Scholars program begins, which will become Langham Partnership International
July 1974	Keynote address at Lausanne Congress; pleads for new balance between evangelism and social action; writes commentary on Lausanne Covenant he has drafted
1975	Becomes Rector Emeritus of All Souls; Michael Baughen becomes rector
November 1975	Adviser at fifth assembly of World Council of Churches First becomes known as 'Uncle John'
Summer 1977	Second visit to South America; visits Galapagos Islands
April to May 1980	In Eastern Europe
1981	Visits India and Bangladesh; meets Mother Teresa
January 1982	London Institute of Contemporary Christianity launched
1984	First edition of *Issues Facing Christians Today* published
1986	*The Cross of Christ* published
July 1989	Lausanne II, Manila, Philippines
August 1989	Sails up Amazon
1992	*The Contemporary Christian* published
1996	*The Message of 1 Timothy and Titus* published, the last of the seven volumes in the Bible Speaks Today series that he wrote himself
May 1998	Embolisms impair eyesight; gives up driving
January to February 1999	With study assistant John Yates to China, Thailand and Hong Kong
1999	*Evangelical Truth* launched at IFES World Assembly
January 31, 2000	With study assistant Corey Widmer in Kenya and Uganda; time with David Zac Niringiye

September 2001	Appoints Chris Wright as his successor as international director of Langham Partnership International
2003	*Why I Am a Christian* published
April 10, 2005	Listed by *Time* magazine as one of 100 most influential people in the world
2006	*Through the Bible, Through the Year* published
2007	*The Living Church* published
June 8, 2007	Moves to College of St. Barnabas, Lingfield, Surrey
July 17, 2007	Preaches at Keswick forty-five years after first visit
2010	*The Radical Disciple* published
July 27, 2011	Dies at the age of ninety